WOODLAND
GARDENS

SHADE GETS CHIC

C. Colston Burrell, Guest Editor

Janet Marinelli
SERIES EDITOR

Anne Witte Garland
ASSOCIATE EDITOR

Bekka Lindstrom
ART DIRECTOR

Stephen K·M. Tim
VICE PRESIDENT, SCIENCE, LIBRARY & PUBLICATIONS

Judith D. Zuk
PRESIDENT

Elizabeth Scholtz
DIRECTOR EMERITUS

Handbook #145

Copyright © Winter 1995 by the Brooklyn Botanic Garden, Inc.

BBG gardening books are published quarterly at 1000 Washington Ave., Brooklyn, NY 11225

Subscription included in Brooklyn Botanic Garden membership dues ($35.00 per year)

ISSN 0362-5850 ISBN # 0-945352-90-5

PRINTED IN KOREA

Table of Contents

INTRODUCTION
Shade Gets Chic

BY C. COLSTON BURRELL

TREES, AND THE SHADE THEY CAST, have often been seen as the bane of gardeners, but they don't have to be. Growing up I learned an important gardening lesson: If you make peace with shade, you will be rewarded with the quiet enchantment of the woodlands.

I was raised on a tree-lined street, but the trees were not in rows. They were in groves and clumps much as they had grown before houses were insinuated among them. There were no sidewalks, no paved driveways and very little lawn. This verdant setting didn't please all the neighbors, however, because where trees grow, lawns lose out. There were those who wouldn't take bare spots in their turf without a fight. They seeded, fertilized and mowed in a vain attempt to recreate the little patches of emerald lawn they found so desirable.

My mother gave up on grass without even trying. She went off to the garden club to find out what would grow in the shade; she was enough of a gardener to know that turf would not. That's how I came to woodland gardening. I came to love woodland plants because that's what we could grow. To this day, despite my love affairs with meadows, prairies and perennial borders, woodland gardens and woodland plants are still my favorites.

Immersed in trees as I was, I came to understand how the forest was structured. I became intimately acquainted with its rhythms. Over the years I watched as it changed. Meanwhile, I was gardening. I experimented with plant combinations, tried new and choice plants, checked soil pH and enjoyed myself immensely. Those lessons are irreplaceable. They have made me the gardener I am today. Some 25 years later, I have designed and cared for shaded gardens of all sizes and descriptions, from grand woodlands to shaded urban lots. The lessons

Shade has long been seen as the bane of gardeners, but it doesn't have to be. Make peace with shade and you'll be rewarded with the quiet enchantment of a woodland garden.

are the same. Many of the problems faced by woodland gardeners are universal: the bare spots under huge lawn trees; the deadly dry shade under conifers; a desire to grow shade plants in an arid climate or in a garden with little or no shade. Some gardeners are faced with too much of a good thing. They may have an existing woodland but don't know where to start. Or, perhaps years of success in the shade have posed the daunting task of reigning in an existing garden that has gotten just a bit too wild.

If you garden under existing trees, you will soon find that massive site manipulations aren't easy. The costs in labor alone are staggering, but the greatest cost may be to the woodland itself. Woodlands and the plants they support exist due to certain conditions of light, soil and water; survival depends on the integrity of the system. Massive undertakings to alter soil pH, change water regimes or open canopies are impractical and ill advised. Instead, it's best to go with what you've got. If your soil is lime based, plant lime-loving species. If you have a xeric oak woodland, grow drought-tolerant plants. I have seen oaks destroyed by over-watering with irrigation systems and trees killed by massive soil removal and replacement.

Minor changes in your garden are okay and often necessary; after all, it is a garden. But go easy: Remove a few low-hanging branches to let in a bit more light. Add a layer of compost to increase the organic content of the soil. Selectively remove a few small trees to avoid overcrowding. Slight pH alterations may

5

be necessary, but try to work to restore the balance rather than set up an artificial system that is bound to fail.

In the pages of this handbook we endeavor to present as complete a picture of the woodland as we can. We start from the top of the canopy and work down to introduce you to the lessons I learned many years ago as a new gardener in a world of trees. Ardent shade gardeners from around the country tell you how they tackled universal problems. Even though their solutions are specific to their regions of the country or particular sites, their methodology can be applied everywhere. You can learn from them how to approach problems and apply the specifics to your own garden.

Remember that the garden is for you as well as for your plants. Place a bench in a cool, quiet recess. This spot will become a treasured venue for learning new lessons from the forest, or just enjoying peace, quiet and a good book. 🌳

Massive undertakings to alter the soil, moisture and light conditions in your backyard woodland are impractical and ill advised. Instead, go with what you've got, creating a delightful tapestry of plants suited to the site.

WOODLAND ECOLOGY

To be a successful woodland gardener, you need to understand the structure of the forest, from the tallest canopy trees to the ferns, wildflowers and carpet of leaves on the forest floor. You need to become acquainted with the forest's rhythms, from the explosion of bloom by ephemeral wildflowers in early spring to the blaze of foliage in the fall. And, because woodlands and the plants they support exist due to certain conditions of light, soil and water, you need to understand the integrity of the entire system. The following primer on woodland ecology will help you work with nature to create a shady garden with style and grace.

COVERED BY CANOPY
The Structure of the Forest

BY ED CLEBSCH

BEFORE YOU BEGIN to garden in the shade, it's important to understand the structure of woodlands, because that structure will dictate how much light reaches the forest floor and will influence water availability and other factors that in turn will guide your choice of plants.

VERTICAL STRUCTURE

Most woodland gardening is either controlled or heavily influenced by the tallest, or canopy, trees; shade gardening is essentially the manipulation of the layers of vegetation under the canopy.

The canopy is made up of all the tree crowns in a given area of forest. Millions of years of evolutionary trial and error have produced two extremes in types of crowns, monolayered and multilayered. Understanding crown structure helps you to evaluate the light conditions under your forest's canopy, or to anticipate the density of shade that would be cast by any tree that you're considering growing in your garden. In monolayered trees, the leaves are arranged close together toward the outside of the crown in a single layer that may be up to several feet thick. Monolayered trees typically occur in the interior of mature forests, and their leaves generally are less lobed or notched than those of multilayer trees. They make the most of the little light available. A branch from a monolayered tree casts substantial shade; as little as 10 percent of the light striking a branch will penetrate below it. Examples are beech, maples, oaks, hickories, spruces and firs. The leaves of multilayered trees, as the name suggests, are arrayed in many layers from the trunk to the outside of the crown. These trees tend to grow in more open areas. Their individual leaves are small and deeply notched or lobed to aid in allowing sunlight to penetrate. Anywhere from 15 to 45 percent of the sunlight manages to penetrate beneath the average branch. This gives many leaves a chance to photosynthesize. Elms, walnuts, hackberry and persimmon are examples of multilayered trees.

The shape of tree crowns—either cone-shaped, fan-shaped or resembling inverted 'U's or circles squeezed from the side—further influences how much light gets close or all the way to the forest floor, where we garden. The crown structure of some kinds of trees changes little over time—for example, some pines and many other conifers. Once these inverted-cone-shaped trees overlap with other individuals they cast dense, year-round shade on the forest floor. As the trees grow, the shade doesn't get any denser; rather, the height at which the branches overlap simply rises as the forest grows. On the other hand, the crown structure of other kinds of trees—tulip trees, for example—does change as they

North America includes some of the planet's most magnificent forests, including the temperate rainforests of the Pacific Northwest.

mature. Tulip tree crowns are shaped like inverted cones during their early and middle years of rapid growth. But when they reach full height the top of the crown rounds out and there is considerable overlap with crowns of adjacent trees. Again, the payoff to the shade gardener is understanding that the crown shapes of various trees will cast varying degrees of shade, which may or may not change over the years, depending on the species. This knowledge will help you choose plants best suited to the light intensities present on your site.

Below the canopy are the plants that grow under the trees, in their shade. Whether they are woody or herbaceous, these small trees, shrubs, herbs, mosses and ferns comprise as many as three distinct vertical layers of foliage in addition to the tree canopy. For the most aesthetically pleasing and ecologically diverse planting, strive to recreate these vertical layers in your garden. Small trees form the *understory*. Shrubs and seedling trees make up the *shrub layer*. Wildflowers, ferns and mosses create a tapestry known as the *ground layer*.

There are two additional vertical layers in forests which, though underground and unseen, profoundly influence the environments in which we garden. Most plants have a root system that is either near the soil surface or that penetrates deeply. Red spruce, for example, tends to have a shallow root system, while its companion species, balsam fir and (in the southern Appalachians) Fraser fir, both are tap-rooted. Some plants have a combination of both systems—for example, sugar maple and longleaf pine. In a natural forest, shallow, fibrous-rooted plants grow next to plants with deep bulbs, which are next to ones with creeping rhizomes. In this eclectic but well-orchestrated arrangement, competition for root space is minimized and more plants can grow together in a limited space. Gardeners can take their cue from nature and create the most diverse planting possible by using species with a variety of root systems. On the other hand, if you're gardening in an existing forest with a very dense surface root system, you may have to remove some potential competitors if you want to add other plants.

DEGREES OF PLANT COVER

The amount of light that reaches the forest floor—and hence the kinds of plants you can grow—is determined not only by the mono- or multilayered structure of individual tree crowns and their shapes but also by how close together the crowns are and how much they overlap. Not all forests are alike in this respect. There may be large gaps in the tree canopy, with spaces between tree crowns larger than the crowns themselves. The once extensive longleaf pine savannas of the southeast states have open canopies, for example, while both the deciduous and coniferous forests of the Northeast had closed canopies before they were exploited intensively by the colonists. Likewise, understory trees like the flowering dogwood and redbud of the eastern forests may have crowns that overlap one another under the forest canopy, or they may be quite scattered. The same applies to the shrub and ground layers. Regardless of

continues on page 14

VERTICAL LAYERS OF THE FOREST

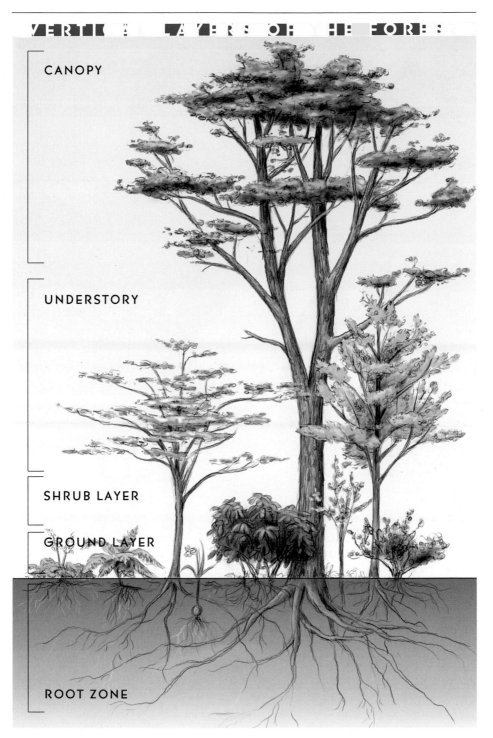

CANOPY

UNDERSTORY

SHRUB LAYER

GROUND LAYER

ROOT ZONE

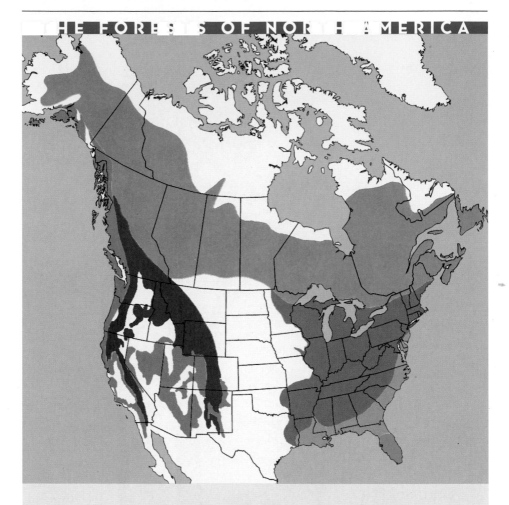

THE FORESTS OF NORTH AMERICA

NORTHERN CONIFER FOREST

EASTERN DECIDUOUS FOREST

PACIFIC COAST CONIFER FOREST

COASTAL PLAIN FOREST

WESTERN MONTANE CONIFER FOREST

SUBTROPICAL FOREST

WESTERN WOODLAND

S tep back in time to the period of the first European colonists and view what is now North America. What kinds of forests would you find? A familiarity with the original forests of your area will provide valuable knowledge on, among other things, climate and soil conditions, as well as the native species that are good potential garden plants. It will also enable you to better predict how well non-native species will fare in your woodland.

Today, although fragments of these forests remain, they have been severely reduced by agriculture and urban development. Along and north of the U.S.-Canadian border, from coast to coast, is a forest of coniferous evergreen trees, once interrupted only by grasslands in the plains states and provinces. This is the boreal forest or taiga. Coniferous trees also dominate the forests at the higher elevations of the Appalachians and most of the Rocky Mountains. High elevations of mountains in the Basin and Range Province, including parts of New Mexico, Arizona, Utah and Nevada, are mantled in pine forests. The lower elevations of the Sierra Nevada and Coast Ranges of California are covered with a complex mosaic of grasslands and savannah, or grassland with widely spaced trees. The western Rocky Mountains, including the tablelands of parts of Colorado, Utah, New Mexico and Arizona, are blanketed with woodlands consisting of widely spaced junipers and pinon pines. Around the Great Lakes the forest is a mixture of Canada hemlock, a needle-leaved evergreen, and a variety of deciduous hardwood tree species.

In the East, from the prairies of the Midwest to the lower western slopes of the Appalachians and east of the mountains from western Georgia to New England, an enormously broad belt of deciduous forests covers the land. This eastern deciduous forest biome itself can be divided into a number of different plant associations in which different species of trees predominate. On the Coastal Plain of the Atlantic and Gulf states, from New Jersey to Texas, the vegetation consists mostly of an open forest of pines, where the crowns of the trees do not overlap and the ground is carpeted with grasses and flowering herbs. The southernmost third of peninsular Florida is another world entirely—a subtropical broad-leaved evergreen forest, fringed by coastal mangrove swamps.

whether any or all the layers overlap or are far apart, they all shade the ground beneath them to some degree. This shading, called "plant cover" or "coverage," profoundly influences light, temperature and moisture conditions. Coverage is usually expressed as a percentage of the ground shaded by the plants above and may be as high as 100 percent in old-growth forests of the Mid-Atlantic and northeastern United States and as low as 50 percent in old-growth longleaf pine forests of the Southeast.

Open forests with low coverage generally have much more light than those with high coverage. Air and surface soil temperatures in open habitats are warmer on sunny days and colder on cloudless nights than those in habitats with higher coverage because there are no leaves to absorb and reflect the sun's radiant energy. What's more, because there are no leaves to intercept rainfall in open habitats, soil surfaces become wet more quickly than those in habitats with higher plant coverage. But they also dry out faster when the sun comes out.

Plant species are limited in their adaptations to light intensity, to extremes of soil moisture and atmospheric humidity, and to extremes of temperature of both air and soil. Plants adapted to the deep shade of coniferous forests—partridgeberry, for example—may perish in the open sun. Conversely, plants that do best in open, sunny habitats, such as sunflowers or bluestem grasses, may perish in deep shade. This is why it's important to choose plants suited to the conditions on your site.

HORIZONTAL STRUCTURE

Light, moisture, slope and soil also directly affect where a plant or group of plants grows in a forest. Plants form horizontal patterns of distribution in response to these factors. Oaks, for example, are found in the relatively dry sites on sunny slopes, while maple and basswood grow in comparatively moist soils on east and north slopes. Good reference books and some nursery catalogs provide solid information on the optimal habitat for any given species. Many species can be grown in environments much different from those in which they're found naturally; bald cypress, sycamore, tree willows, mallows and yellow flag iris are all normally associated with wet habitats and yet grow well in surprisingly dry habitats as well. To test the tolerance of a particular plant without some degree of caution or long (and expensive) experience by trial and error is to court failure, however. Success at woodland gardening requires that you know the habitat requirements of your chosen plants.

THE NATURE OF FOREST SOILS

The soil is the substrate upon which all forest life depends. Soil is a source of mechanical support for plants, in addition to being a source of oxygen, nutrients and water. Loose, dry sands, for example, could not provide mechanical support for a tree that weighs several tons and is subjected to the force of wind.

The characteristics of a soil at a given place are determined by the combined effects over time of the underlying geology or bedrock and its continual erosion, climate, including rainfall, and vegetation and other organisms. Geology provides the basic elemental material. Soil particles come in three size categories,

Small-leaved trees like aspen form an open canopy that casts light or dappled shade. Wildflowers adapted to such an open forest may not do well in the dense shade of spruces, firs, maples and oaks.

the mixture of which gives soil its texture. Sand grains are the largest soil particles, followed by silt particles and microscopic-sized clay particles. Good healthy soils are a mixture of sand, silt and clay and are called loams. Coastal soils, because they are geologically quite young, are largely sandy. Clay soils are most common in the South, where rainfall is highest. Sandy soils, with their large sand grains, are well aerated, as oxygen has no difficulty penetrating among the particles. However, water also moves very quickly through sand, making sandy soils prone to drought. In contrast, clay soils become very tightly packed because the microscopic clay particles tend to stick together. Therefore, clay soils are often poorly aerated and water logged.

Forests fall into three basic categories according to the amount of moisture present. A plant adapted to a dry habitat is usually not well suited to survive in a wet one, and vice versa. Mesic forests occur on well-drained soils, usually loams. These forests typically are very diverse, with many different species of trees and other plants, and they generally look quite lush. Xeric forests occur on sandy soils that are usually overly dry. Forests of the Coastal Plain, for example, are xeric. In northern regions, south-facing mountain slopes also are often xeric both because soils are thin on mountain slopes and because high levels of sunshine result in warmer temperatures and the potential for water stress. Hydric forests, commonly called swamps, occur in low-lying areas that retain water. These forests are constantly moist and the soil is usually water logged.

The spaces between and around mineral grains are occupied not only by water or air, but also by dead organic matter and living organisms, including microbes, tiny animals and living roots. The water that drains through soils carries dissolved material with it, including dissolved chemicals, the nutrients that plants utilize. Most of these nutrients are returned to the soil when the plants die and decay. Plant litter also contains organic matter, which aerates soil and improves its ability to retain water as well as dissolved nutrient ions, providing a more stable supply of nutrients to plant roots.

Soil pH, another important factor that will dictate your choice of plants, is determined to a large degree by an area's geology. Precipitation adds to the acidity of the soil; therefore, slightly acidic soils are the norm in regions of high precipitation. Conifer needles and many deciduous leaves also add to the acidity of the soil when they decompose.

It is possible to manipulate many of these soil characteristics with various amendments and by tilling to create the optimum conditions for the plants you want to grow. The wisest course of action ecologically, however, is to work with your existing soil and choose the plants best suited to it.

From Spring Wildflowers to Fall Foliage

BY C. COLSTON BURRELL

CHANGE IS THE RULE in forests. From earliest spring, when the buds of trees begin to swell, until a carpet of newly fallen leaves provides protection from winter cold, the woodland changes with each passing day.

Spring sunshine pours through the bare branches of the trees and warms the forest floor. After winter's dormancy, buds of wildflowers are set to burst into life. Some of them, such as spring beauty and false rue anemone, may have produced foliage during winter's warm spells. As the days lengthen and the sun begins to prevail, an explosion of growth occurs. Over just a few weeks' time, the

Some spectacular woodland wildflowers such as *Trillium grandiflorum* are notoriously slow to propagate and are therefore often collected from the wild and sold. Buy plants only if you're sure they have been nursery propagated.

forest floor is transformed into a spectacular display of wildflowers rivaling that of any prairie or alpine meadow.

Nowhere is the display of spring wildflowers more spectacular than in the deciduous forests of eastern and central North America. This extravagant, flamboyant explosion of blooms is celebrated across the land, especially in the mountains, with festivals and field trips. The wildflower pilgrimage to the Smoky Mountains is legendary. People come from all over the world for lectures, workshops and tours, or just to hike and enjoy the spectacle. The wildflowers produce such a dramatic show because their bloom cycles are tied to the availability of light and moisture. The spring woods, moist with winter's precipitation, are flooded with light, but summer's leafy trees will rob the forest floor of all but filtered light. Wildflowers must take advantage of this narrow window of time to grow and reproduce.

After a few weeks of gloriously warm weather, tree buds break and the burst of leaf growth begins to form a veil of shade on the forest floor. The veil quickly changes into dappled shade as the leaves expand. Within a few short weeks the canopy provides a coverlet of cooling shade. Light levels fall to a consistent level, where they remain for the duration of the summer. By the time the canopy closes in, a textural carpet of green—ferns, mosses and the foliage of herbaceous plants—is all that remains.

The seasonal change in the forest canopy is echoed by the plants that grow underneath. Consider cinnamon fern as an example. In early spring, the fern uses energy stored in its rhizome to push up fresh fiddleheads. The fronds gradually broaden and mature as the forest canopy closes in. When the fronds are fully mature they form huge solar collectors to make maximum use of the dim light in the shaded recesses of the forest. By autumn, the fronds lie golden brown in the earliest frost.

EARLY BLOOMERS

Each plant in the forest has a slightly different strategy for survival. Blooming and setting seed are exhausting jobs for plants. Lots of energy is required, energy that comes from the sun. Most forest wildflowers grow and bloom early to maximize their potential to regain the energy expended plus store sufficient reserves to do it all again the following year. For gardeners, this means a glorious springtime flower display. Garden making is almost *too* easy with such excess. But it's important to keep in mind that many early-blooming wildflowers are ephemeral. Ephemeral means short lived, and refers to the fact that these plants go dormant soon after blooming. As soon as seed is ripe, the plants die back for the season, thereby conserving their resources. This strategy developed because the woods become shaded and dry in summer and foliage is a liability for a small, delicate wildflower. In addition to pressures from trees, the smaller, early plants will be overtopped by taller plants that grow later in the season. Early dormancy helps to avoid competition between a dainty Dutchman's breeches and a churlish spike-nard, which may grow to four feet with an equal spread.

Because so many early bloomers are ephemeral, beware a woodland garden built on spring wildflowers alone. If you plant only ephemerals, by June all that remains is bare soil. Use a variety of wildflowers and ferns to create a display that lasts all season long.

Spring-blooming wildflowers exploit one of two strategies to insure success in the woodland environment. The most common adaptation to this season's

A glorious woodland garden with primroses in full spring bloom.

ROOT TYPES

Corms, bulbs or tuberous roots enable plants to resist drought and store food. Many ephemeral woodland wildflowers have such underground food-storage structures to provide the energy needed for rapid leaf and flower development in early spring.

FIBROUS ROOT An unmodified or typical root radiating from a crown. Anchors the plant and absorbs water and nutrients. Examples: merrybells, foamflower, hepatica and grasses.

TUBEROUS ROOT A thickened fibrous root modified for water and nutrient storage. Example: Virginia bluebell.

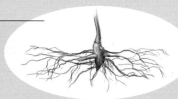

CORM A modified stem base for food storage, swollen like a bulb. Example: Jack-in-the-pulpit.

BULB A modified stem for food storage consisting of thickened modified leaves. Examples: lilies and trout lily.

RHIZOME A modified horizontal stem for food and water storage that roots at the nodes and produces new growth annually at the distal ends. Examples: trillium and Solomon's-seal.

TUBER A modified underground stem for food and water storage with nodes called eyes. Example: spring beauty.

20

rhythm is to store energy for quick growth. Ephemeral wildflowers such as spring beauty, toothwort and Dutchman's breeches have underground storage structures such as tubers, bulbs, rhizomes and corms to provide the energy needed for rapid leaf and flower development (see "Root Types," opposite). Stored reserves fuel the plant so it can spread its leaves while the sun is still available, allowing it to produce the food to sustain seed production and to store enough reserves for next spring.

Persistent wildflowers such as trillium, bloodroot and wild geranium use the same quick-growth strategy nourished by specialized underground storage structures. But instead of going dormant, they spread wide foliage to garner every bit of light that falls on their piece of ground. In a dry year, or when competition with other plants gets too tough, they may go dormant at any time if their foliage becomes a liability. Some spring wildflowers keep their foliage all through the summer and even turn bright colors in the autumn, adding to the foliage and fruit displays of the woody plants above them.

This combination of adaptive strategies allows many plants to grow in close proximity in the wild. Plants partition both the above- and below-ground environments. Gardeners can exploit this natural pattern to create stunning combinations of plants. Ephemerals such as spring beauty, with their compact bulbs, can be grown alongside persistent, fibrous-rooted wild geranium, which in turn can be planted with a tall fern. The ground under all these plants can be carpeted with shallow-rooted, evergreen partridgeberry. The spring beauty will push up through the ground-hugging partridgeberry in early spring, spreading its delicate foliage just a few inches high. As its seed is ripening and growth is waning, tall wild geranium is extending its stems and beginning to bloom. Meanwhile, the fern is also expanding its fronds. When the fern is mature, the spring beauty will be but a memory. Once you understand the individual rhythms of wildflowers, you can compose a garden tapestry that offers continual exhilaration.

Small plants need alternate tactics for insuring adequate food production and storage. A second common strategy for survival that woodland wildflowers employ is evergreen foliage. The advantage of evergreen leaves is that they are tough and leathery so they can endure dry spells. Because they are always green, they can produce food from early spring until hard frost, or whenever the temperature is above 45°F. Plants such as hepatica, partridgeberry and bunchberry fall into this group. Many of these evergreen plants are native to mixed deciduous and evergreen woodlands and to boreal zones where their evergreen leaves help them cope with year-round shade (see the discussion of coniferous forests that follows).

LATE BLOOMERS

The spring ephemerals often raise their foliage only a few inches above the leaf litter. As they are going dormant, taller ferns, merrybells and other persistent plants are taking their space. Late-blooming plants produce a flush of lush foliage early in the year, spreading broad leaves, and growing steadily through the seasons, overlooked by most gardeners. As our eyes are riveted on the early wildflowers, the foliage of these late bloomers is producing and storing energy in preparation for late summer and autumn flowering. As the season wears on, the bloom stalks elongate, lifting the foliage closer to the light source. As summer wanes, the forest blossoms anew. Asters, goldenrods and grasses are the dominant blooms now. Their rich golden and sky-blue flowers portend the autumnal spectacle to come.

The late blooms are augmented by a profusion of berries. The dusty cobalt of blue cohosh, the porcelain white of baneberry and the grape-like clusters of spikenard add to the colorful display. Berries do double duty, providing a feast for our eyes and for the stomachs of wildlife.

THE AUTUMN LEAVES

As autumn approaches, the trees relinquish summer's trappings. A portion of the stored energy of the sun is returned to the earth in a rain of blazing foliage. The fall foliage display in the eastern deciduous forest is every bit as spectacular as the spring wildflower display. Travelers worldwide set their sights on New England and other leafy destinations for tours by train, bus and car, or quiet hikes in the colorful countryside. By planning for autumn foliage as carefully as for spring wildflowers, you can witness the same spectacle in your own backyard.

The red and burgundy shades of dogwood and sumac are the first to appear. The golden birches and blazing maples are next. Oaks carry the display into early winter. Each species has a unique range of colors. Hickories turn bright yellow; red maple fiery red; sugar maple flaming orange; and red oak deep burgundy.

Trees are not alone in this onslaught of color. Deciduous shrubs have an equally dazzling array of leaf colors as well as brilliant displays of red, purple and black fruits. These persistent berries extend the show into winter, ornamenting bare branches as snow falls. Birds and other wildlife depend on the berries for food, taking each type in turn when its sugar content is highest and it is most palatable. Wildflowers such as wild geranium are not upstaged, their leaves turning shades of wine and rose.

Autumn foliage has ecological as well as aesthetic benefits. Most of the nutrients in the forest are tied up in the plants themselves. When trees and shrubs lose their leaves, they return nutrients to the soil. Decay and nutrient release are slow, so plants have a steady supply of food. This annual renewal is essential not only for the forest's nutrient cycle, but also for providing winter mulch to prevent rapid temperature change in the soil and thus to protect tender plants and delicate crowns from drying winter winds.

The fall foliage display in the eastern deciduous forest is every bit as beautiful as the spring wildflower spectacle. Plan for autumn foliage as carefully as for spring blooms.

CONIFEROUS FORESTS

Forests dominated by coniferous trees are ruled by different rhythms. Year-round shade is often dense. The tall trunks and narrow, cone-shaped crowns allow conifers to grow close together, effectively blocking most direct rays from the sun. Pine forests are the most open canopied of the conifer forests; some direct sun reaches the forest floor during the day. Spruce, Douglas fir and hemlock forests are the darkest. Little or no direct sun actually falls on the duff-covered earth.

As an adaptation to year-round shade, plants bring out the heavy artillery—thick, evergreen leaves. Persistent leaves enable plants to photosynthesize all season long. Evergreen leaves are leathery to help plants resist drought. Evergreen needles are effective barriers that prevent rainfall from reaching the ground. Much of the precipitation in northern and western forests evaporates directly from the canopy without ever reaching the forest floor. Because less water reaches the ground, plants have to be drought tolerant. Make sure you select ground layer plants suited to the lack of moisture in these forests. Confine plants that need consistently moist soils to low spots and streamsides.

Coniferous trees are often found in cooler areas, either at northern latitudes or at higher elevations. Western forests receive a large proportion of annual precipitation as snow. Summer rainfall is periodic and often scarce, especially on the east slope of the Rockies. In other areas, such as the pine barrens of Long Island and New Jersey as well as portions of the southern coastal plain, evergreens replace deciduous trees where drought cycles or fire limit the number and diversity of deciduous species. Shrubs and herbs respond to these conditions as well. Many western shrubs have leathery or hairy leaves to help conserve water. Wildflowers utilize bulbs, taproots or other means to help them cope.

Bloom in coniferous forests is geared less to sun and light patterns and more to temperature and moisture. Soil thaws and warms slowly in shade. As the snow melts, the earliest plants bloom, but the main show is spread between late spring and summer. Deciduous plants bloom first. As in deciduous forests, they expand quickly to make the most of the season. Wildflowers that require higher light levels are confined to the edges of woodlands, or to younger forests of deciduous pioneer species such as birch and alder. Evergreen species bloom later. A few deciduous asters bloom in the autumn, before winter's snow blankets the ground, resetting the clock and beginning the sequence anew.

Gardening in the Shade

BY F M MOOBERRY

Success with a woodland garden requires some attention to the basic requirements of light and soil, proper plant selection and planting and some commonsense maintenance. It is not difficult and is well worth the effort.

As a first step to starting a garden, inventory what is already growing on the site. Are the trees deciduous or evergreen? Is there an understory of shrubs? If not, you may want to plant one. A close examination of existing growth may show desirable species that you want to save. If invasive non-natives have taken over, they must be controlled before you establish your garden (see "Maintaining Your Woodland Garden," page 33). Hand weeding is safest because it will do the least damage to plants you want to preserve, including trees and shrubs.

LIGHT AND SHADE

Available light determines the difference between an open meadow and a woodland garden. Woodland plants require partial or filtered sunlight for most of the day. Trees and shrubs provide the sheltering canopy but you need to understand what kind of light you have, and how to manipulate light and shade to achieve the optimum conditions for what you want to grow.

Different plants require or tolerate different degrees of shade. Gardening books provide guidelines for different species based on broad categories of dense, dappled or partial shade.

Dense shade is created by large trees such as maples, oaks and hickories with thick canopies and overlapping leaves.

Light or dappled shade is provided by an open canopy of small-leaved trees such as birch and locust.

A meandering path heightens the tranquil charm of a woodland garden. When creating your woodland walk, mimic the way that streams wind through a forest floor.

Partial shade means about half a day of sun and half of shade, as you would find at a woodland edge.

Light is also influenced by topography. For example, a south-facing slope receives much more light than a northern slope. What time of day your woodland garden receives direct sunlight is also important. Temperatures increase in the afternoon. Many plants require protection from the heat and the sun's burning rays at this time of day.

Sun and shade patterns differ with each woodland. Study and record the ones in your garden. The morning patterns will be different from those in the afternoon. What's more, because the sun's track changes during the year, spring sun and shade will be different from summer's. Shade patterns at the edge of the woodland should also be noted. Edges allow light to penetrate farther into the woods, even under large canopy trees. Record your findings in a notebook, along with simple sketches; these will become important tools for the planning of your garden, refreshing your memory as the process may continue over a considerable period of time.

MANIPULATING SHADE

Even the most shade-tolerant plants often benefit from a bit more light. Too much shade can be corrected by pruning existing vegetation to allow light into the garden. I suggest that you prune on a sunny day when the trees are in full leaf and you can see the results immediately. If you're doing the work yourself you have the luxury of pruning over several growing seasons. Taking down a quarter of the branches at a time will avoid an overly severe thinning. Removing some of the major branches of large trees is a dangerous job best left to professionals. To keep down costs, you'll probably need to have this type of thinning done all at once.

The quickest way to provide additional shade if you have too much sun is to plant young trees and a dense secondary layer of shrubs. It is important to choose shrubs that will thrive in full sun when they are first planted. These sun-loving shrubs will decline in vigor as the trees grow and the shade canopy increases. Many different kinds of shrubs are available at local garden centers and nurseries. Most shrubs are fast growing and can be pruned up to provide a quick shade canopy. As your larger trees mature the shrubs can be pruned, thinned or removed altogether. (For more on creating shade from scratch, see page 42.)

SOIL

In addition to light and shade the selection of appropriate plant species should be guided by the drainage and soil characteristics in your yard. Instead of trying to change existing conditions, match your plants to the site—it's not only easier on the environment but also a lot less work for you. Most woodland plants will benefit from a rich soil that insures good air circulation, water and nutrient retention and drainage. Shade-loving plants also favor loose-textured soils, which promote deeper, more drought-resistent roots. Organic matter is the key. It mod-

For best success, look to your local woods for ideas on plants best adapted to the soils in your area. Rhododendrons, azaleas and other acid-loving plants thrive when the soil pH is around 5.5.

ifies sandy soils to improve moisture retention and breaks up clay soils to add structure and reduce moisture retention. As it breaks down, the organic matter also slowly releases plant nutrients. Unlike herbaceous plants, trees and shrubs become established and grow better in the original soil, without amendments other than a surface layer of compost.

A simple test will determine the composition of your soil. Put 2 cups of soil taken from the top 6 to 8 inches of your garden into a clear glass quart jar. Fill with water, cap and shake vigorously. Wait 24 hours. The organic material will be the layer floating on the surface; the next layer is clay; the third layer, silt; and the bottom layer, sand. This profile will show you what basic materials you have and their relative proportions. A perfect soil for a woodland garden would have a small percentage of clay and sand and a large proportion of silt and organic matter.

Test the site for drainage by filling a hole with water. If there is still standing water after six hours, choose plants that thrive in wet soil.

Soil chemistry, particularly soil pH (the degree of acidity and alkalinity), is another consideration. For best success, look to your local woods for ideas on which plants are adapted to the soils in your area. The pH scale ranges from 0 to 14. The lower the number, the more acid; 7 is neutral; and high numbers are alkaline. Most eastern soils tend to be acidic, while midwestern and western soils are neutral to slightly alkaline. Most commercially available woodland plants grow best in slightly acid soil with a pH of 6 to 6.5. Azaleas, rhododen-

If there's any "miracle ingredient" for a woodland garden, it's mulch. Nature renews the mulch in forests each year as plants lose their leaves. Woodland gardens likewise benefit from an annual application of leaf mulch, typically in the fall.

drons and blueberries thrive when the soil pH is around 5.5. Plants from regions with limestone bedrock do best in the range of 6.8 to 7.2. Red osier dogwood, staghorn sumac and native viburnums such as cranberry and arrowwood are shrubs that do well in alkaline soil.

You can purchase simple soil-testing kits from local garden supply outlets. You can also get a complete soil chemistry profile from your county's Cooperative Extension office for a small fee.

PLANTING

Spring is a great time to plant because temperatures are cool and rainfall is abundant. Roots have a chance to become established before it gets hot and dry. Fall is also a good time to plant; even after air temperatures drop, the soil remains warm, promoting rapid root growth. Transplant in the morning or evening to avoid stress from strong sunlight and the usually heavier midday winds.

The planting hole should be two to three times the diameter of the root ball but no deeper than the roots. Cover the plant with soil to the level the plants grew at the nursery, which you'll be able to see by a change of color on the stem. (Rhododendrons are shallow rooted, so take care not to set them in too deeply.) Water to eliminate air pockets and settle the soil. Don't step on the roots; rather, firm the soil with your hands. Use the excess soil to build up a small dike around the plant to retain water. Make sure your new transplants receive about an inch of water a week, whether from rain or hand irrigation, until they are established. Apply mulch to help keep the soil moist and keep down weeds.

Plants, especially trees and shrubs, are usually available in three forms: container grown, balled-and-burlaped and bare root.

Container-grown plants. Container-grown plants are the most popular because they can be planted at any time during the growing season. Buy specimens in leaf so you know they are healthy. Try to avoid plants that are rootbound—that is, whose roots have completely filled the container and are wrapped around the bottom; unless you untangle the roots and spread them out they will continue to grow in a circle, never branching out.

When you're ready to transplant, remove the plant by tapping the bottom of the container; then lay the container on its side and pull the stems gently. Spread out the roots if necessary and position the crown at the proper level in the hole. If you have a flat of plants whose roots are intermingled into a solid mass, use a sharp knife and a spatula and cut out plants as you would cut a cake.

Most herbaceous woodland plants benefit from the addition of organic matter at planting time. Trees and shrubs grow better in the original soil, with no amendments other than a surface layer of compost.

Balled-and-burlaped plants. Many shrubs and small trees are available as balled-and-burlaped (B&B) stock. These are dug up with a quantity of the soil around the roots, then tightly wrapped in burlap or other material for transport and handling. A high percentage of the roots in a B&B plant have been cut away but those that are left are safely protected in soil, so be careful not to break up the root ball. Remove the burlap or other wrapping material just before you're ready to plant.

Bare root plants. Bare root plants are available only in early spring and late autumn because they must be dug up when dormant. The nursery will send them at the appropriate time for your region. Put them in as soon as they arrive or, if that's impossible, "heel" them in by placing the plants on their sides and covering the roots with good garden soil. Keep them moist until planted. Soak bare-root plants in a bucket of water for two hours before planting; trim off any broken roots and spread out the roots in the hole.

MULCH

If there's any "miracle ingredient" for a woodland garden, it's mulch. Organic mulches help improve soil structure as they break down over time. Mulch also inhibits the germination of weed seeds and weed growth, reduces the stress on plants by keeping down summer soil temperatures, protects against the winter freeze-thaw cycles that damage plants by keeping soil temperatures relatively constant, and conserves water.

Nature renews the mulch in woodlands each autumn as the plants lose their leaves. Woodland gardens likewise benefit from an annual application of leaf mulch in the fall. Fallen leaves become a valuable asset rather than a disposal problem. Shred or run the lawn mower over the leaves several times before applying them.

Other traditional garden mulches include pine needles, wood chips and shredded bark. Some more exotic materials that make good mulch are locally available, including buckwheat hulls, peanut shells, ground corncobs, cocoa hulls and licorice root. Eight to ten sheets of newspaper placed under mulch is especially effective in creating a weed barrier for new gardens.

Some materials are not recommended. Avoid using salt marsh hay and southern pine straw, as they are removed from native habitats where they are needed to support the natural system. Peat moss not only is extracted from bogs but also forms an impenetrable crust that repels precious water. Hay usually contains weed seeds. Green grass clippings soon turn into a hot smelly mess; leave them on the lawn where they break down, becoming a mild form of fertilizer.

Don't overdo the mulching. Organic mulch applied too thickly allows roots to grow into it. In hot, dry weather these fragile roots can burn and die. This is especially true of trees and shrubs. A good rule of thumb is to apply 3 to 6 inches of mulch and inspect it several time a year for root growth. And keep mulch away from the base of trees and shrubs, as constant moisture in such close proximity can encourage fungus build-up, rotting the bark.

As long as you're using organic mulch annually, synthetic fertilizers will be unnecessary.

Understanding and Managing Vegetation Change

BY GLENN DOUGLAS DREYER

FORESTS, like other plant communities, are dynamic entities that change over time. The changes are caused by the establishment, growth and death of the species that live in the forest and their reactions to site conditions and various kinds of disturbances. Understanding these changes will allow you to anticipate how your garden will evolve, and to some extent shape the process. As your woodland matures, transformations—some subtle, some quite dramatic—will occur.

Keeping the basic structure of the forest canopy intact is critical to successful woodland gardening. Help along at least a few saplings of the tree species that you wish to become the main canopy members in the future.

SUCCESSION AND CLIMAX

"Succession" and "climax" are the two classic terms used to describe vegetation change over time. Popularized by American ecologist Frederick Clements early in this century, these concepts were very useful in getting scientists thinking and talking about change in natural systems. But we now realize that they were gross oversimplifications.

Succession was originally used to describe a process in which vegetation changes in a plant community are inherent in the community itself; outside factors such as storms or fire were thought to be of little or no importance in this process. The changes were believed to unfold in an orderly, predictable manner, with each group of plants preparing the way for the next. According to this theory, different associations of plants colonize in waves. Eventually, the community reaches an end point, the climax, which is stable and self-perpetuating for long periods of time.

We now know that a wide variety of vegetation types can be relatively stable, persisting for what seems to humans like a long time. But these are not necessarily end points of some successional sequence. For example, the Hempstead Plains, located just east of New York City, was a 50-square-mile grassland in the eastern deciduous forest. (All but a few acres are now under houses and asphalt.) Here, very dry, sandy soils, combined with frequent fires, perpetuated this plant community for millennia, preventing it from becoming forest.

It is now clear that a number of different processes cause vegetation change, and it is a much more complex and less predictable phenomenon than was originally thought. For example, far from making it easy for other plants to become established, many species actually inhibit the invasion of their space by competing with them for resources and, in some cases, by allelopathy—that is, by excreting a chemical or chemicals toxic to other plants.

DISTURBANCE

One of the most important recent ecological insights is the critical role of periodic disturbance—fire, flooding, insects, windstorms, to name a few—in maintaining species and habitat diversity. Rather than an anomaly that occasionally disrupts climax communities, disturbance is now viewed as the key recurring factor that keeps a mosaic of habitats in different stages of vegetation development in fairly close proximity to one another. This, in turn, assures the presence of the plants and animals that characterize each phase of the change from open land to mature forest.

When you garden in a woodland, *you* become an agent of disturbance as well. If you want your efforts to have the outcome you desire, it's important to understand whether they work with or contradict natural processes.

Although *how* vegetation succession or change occurs is more complicated than previously thought, *what* will ultimately happen in most places is still generally predictable. It certainly is true that trees will eventually predominate on most sites in forested regions. In the eastern deciduous forests, for example, natural succession on abandoned farmland left undisturbed for 50 or 75 years will work something like this, with regional variations: Millions of seeds that lay dormant in the exposed soil germinate, causing an explosion of physiologically tough, aggressive annuals like horseweed and common ragweed, which dominate the first season. In a few years, biennials (today, many of them non-natives such as common mullein and Queen Anne's lace) become obvious, along with a few perennial wildflowers like asters and goldenrods. After five years or so, the

Periodic disturbances such as windstorms or fire promote biodiversity by creating a mosaic of habitats in different stages of vegetation development.

Some trees live longer, on average, than others. Oaks, above, beeches and firs are among the species that can become centuries old.

meadow is in full bloom with a variety of perennial wildflowers complementing the biennials, interspersed with big bluestem, little bluestem and other native grasses. Within a few years young maples, ashes, dogwoods, cherries, crabapples, pines and cedars, often present early on but inconspicuous, rapidly transform the meadow into "old field," an extremely rich, floriferous blend of pioneer trees, shrubs and herbaceous species particularly favored by wildlife. As the taller trees mature they shade out the grasses, wildflowers and shrubs, and the land becomes forest. Given enough time without disturbance, perhaps several centuries, a mature or old-growth forest might even develop.

Each stage in the field-to-forest continuum offers a different growing environment for plants. For best success, be sure to select plants suited to the particular conditions your woodland provides. It's obvious that a meadow is different from a forest, but even the various stages of forest succession produce different growing conditions. Young woodlands are relatively bright because pioneer species (those sun-loving plants that colonize an area first) are smaller in stature, have smaller leaves and a more open canopy structure. The understory and shrub layers typically become thick, luxuriating in the filtered light.

Eventually, the pioneer plants are overtopped by the canopy species of the mature forest and, as the shade deepens, they decline and die, building a thicker layer of organic matter. In a mature forest, the huge canopy trees filter out much of the summer sun. More shade-tolerant plants take over the forest floor. There is a deep layer of organic matter, making the soil rich. Each stage in the life of a forest offers gardeners both opportunities and challenges.

Disturbances that occur fairly regularly result in communities of plants and animals that are adapted to the disturbance—for example, the Hempstead Plains grassland mentioned earlier and the jack pine forests of the northern Great Lakes would both become oak-dominated forests without periodic fires. On the other hand, a highly unpredictable disturbance— say the sudden incursion of a species new to the community, such as the gypsy moth—can cause short-term havoc.

Disturbance occurs as regularly in the woodland garden as it does in a native forest. That's why it's important, when dealing with either type of ecological system, to consider the matter of scale, both in time and space. In a huge tract of native forest, disturbance—say, trees downed by a major storm—is rarely as disruptive, biologically or aesthetically, as in a garden. Depending on the magnitude of the disturbance, a native forest will recover over a period of decades or

Birches are relatively short lived. If your canopy is dominated by short-lived trees, nurture or plant longer-lived species in the understory.

37

centuries. Knowing that in 20 or 30 years trees downed by a hurricane will be replaced by nature is little consolation to a gardener who wants to enjoy a beautiful and ecologically diverse woodland during his or her lifetime on a piece of property that is a few acres or less.

VEGETATION CHANGE AND THE GARDEN

This section tells you how to evaluate and manage the kinds of disturbance most apt to affect your woodland garden. Changes can result from a number of biological and physical factors. Here's what you can do about some of the major ones.

Protect the canopy of your woodland. Keeping the basic structure of the forest canopy intact is obviously critical to successful woodland gardening—a canopy is by definition what makes a woodland a woodland. Although trees are relatively long-lived organisms, it's important to look ahead. It's wise to help along at least a few of the understory saplings of the trees that you wish to become main canopy members in the future. Selecting and favoring the healthier ones, especially in openings, is a sound management strategy.

It's impossible to predict how long an individual tree will live, but we do know that some species live longer than others, on average. Birch and aspen are relatively short lived, having life spans measured in decades, whereas species like oak, beech or Douglas fir can become centuries old. If your canopy is dominated by short-lived trees, you would do well either to encourage the growth of longer-lived species in the understory or plant some young trees as an eventual replacement overstory.

Non-biological change in the forest canopy is most often due to storm damage. On a regional scale, wind or lightning damage create a mosaic of openings or gaps, increasing the diversity of habitats. But on the scale of your backyard woodland garden, their effects can be devastating. About the only thing you can do is clean up the mess, and work toward restoring the tree canopy as quickly as possible.

Remove invasive species, both native and non-native. Unwanted plants may gain a foothold in the understory of your forest patch and in time may outcompete more desirable plantings. Suckering or clonal trees like sassafras and black locust, aggressively spreading wildflowers like white wood aster and ferns, including hay-scented, are native species that often overwhelm their less competitive neighbors in New England. While they don't affect the dominant canopy trees, they can significantly alter the ground layer and stymie your gardening efforts.

Shade-tolerant non-native species, many of which have escaped from gardens and become naturalized, can also cause rapid and undesirable changes in woodland gardens. Without natural predators, parasites and competitors to restrain

Disease and insects are ever-present agents of change in biological systems. Don't get worked up about some damaged leaves, but consider intervening when a problem threatens your plant's survival. Or consider the loss of one plant an opportunity to try another.

them, these plants can become destructive pests. In every region of North America there are numerous examples of aggressively spreading shrubs, vines, trees and herbaceous plants, imported from distant lands, that are wreaking havoc with forest ecosystems—and woodland gardens. One well known example is the Norway maple (*Acer platanoides*), a European tree introduced to North America during the Colonial period. Used as the primary replacement for American elms killed by Dutch elm disease, Norway maple is the most over-planted tree in the United States. With the help of a tremendous seed supply from urban and suburban plantings, coupled with its shade tolerance, this exotic has begun naturalizing in forests and woodlands throughout the eastern part of the country. Perhaps the saddest case of Norway maple invasion is its predominance in the understory of New Jersey's last remnant of old growth forest, Rutgers University's Metlers Woods.

The only effective way to deal with these aggressive species is to recognize them early on and remove them as they appear. Keep an eye on newcomers to your garden, using field guides to identify them. The native plant society or department of natural resources in your state probably publishes lists of the worst invasive exotics in your area. Use this information to determine whether any newcomer is an appropriate resident. If it isn't, dig it up and destroy it. If you wait until the invaders are well established, drastic removal measures will probably be necessary.

Nurture welcome "volunteers." Natural processes will also introduce many interesting and desirable newcomers to your woodland. These plants should also be identified; perhaps with some encouragement they can bring welcome changes to your garden. A great deal of the charm and distinctive personality of a woodland garden results from the chance establishment of a variety of native plants.

Control damage by deer and other animals. Animals can often cause dramatic, and sometimes rapid, changes in a forested setting. Populations of various species of deer have exploded in recent decades from coast to coast. As the number of deer increase in natural areas, forest regeneration is impeded; plant species most favored by the animals are especially hard hit. The wild herds wander into suburban areas, decimating many garden plants. In fact, our domestic landscapes are a veritable buffet dinner for these hungry herbivores. Browse lines, four to five feet above ground at the upper limit of the deers' reach, are an all-too-familiar site.

Other upland species, like rabbit and ground squirrel, also can cause changes in the species composition of your woodland garden by browsing, burrowing and other activities. The damming of streams by beavers can lead to the demise of a nearby forest by raising the water level by feet—or sometimes only inches.

Changes caused by animals are often extremely difficult to manage. Fencing is the most effective, though expensive, solution.

Consider taking steps to control insects and diseases when they threaten the survival of your plants. Insects and disease are ever-present agents of change in biological systems. Oak wilt, gypsy moth caterpillars, spruce bud worm and lately dogwood anthracnose and hemlock woolly adelgid are only some of the better known problems with which gardeners, foresters and ecologists must contend.

While under natural forest conditions insects and disease are part of a normal disturbance regime and can actually favor biological diversity, in small gardens they're potentially disastrous. The demise of your prized flowering dogwood, for instance, can be heartbreaking. In the woodland garden, as in any garden, let common sense be your guide in matters of insect and disease control. Don't get overly worked up about a few damaged leaves, but consider intervention when a problem threatens the health or survival of your plants. Or, consider the loss of one plant as an opportunity to try another.

It's important to recognize that forests are dynamic, ever-changing systems. Your woodland garden can be a great source of satisfaction if you stay flexible, observing, guiding and at times even celebrating the spontaneous unfolding of nature.

WOODLAND GARDENS

Many of the problems faced by woodland gardeners are universal: the bare spots under huge lawn trees; the deadly dry shade under conifers; the difficulty of growing delicate forest wildflowers in an arid climate or in a garden with little or no shade; or the daunting task of reigning in an existing woodland or garden that's gotten just a bit too wild over the years. In the pages that follow, veteran shade gardeners tell how they have coped with these challenges. Even though their solutions may be specific to their regions of the country or particular sites, their methodology can be applied in your yard, too.

SHADE FROM SCRATCH

Creating a Woodland Garden in the City or Suburbs

BY BRENDA SKARPHOL

CREATING A WOODLAND GARDEN in many suburbs and cities means starting from scratch to create shade. In the city most vegetation of any kind may be long gone; in the suburbs trees may have been bulldozed to make way for development or, in areas where forests don't grow naturally, may never have been there.

Growing up on the open plains with the expansive sky of North Dakota made me appreciate trees. Trees provide a sheltering umbrella during hot summer days, and mute harsh summer light to a verdant, luminous quality. They create an incomparable sense of place and enclosure as well as valuable habitat for wildlife. Today, in my own small suburban yard in Maryland, I value both sunny and shady spaces. My front yard bakes in the southern sun. My backyard, in contrast, moves from full sun to light shade. Some of the shade comes from a grand old willow oak that reaches across from a neighbor's yard; I've added to this by planting other small- to medium-sized trees for screening and seasonal interest.

If you're starting a shade garden from scratch, without mature trees, you can create shade quickly by building arbors. Sun-loving vines growing on these structures cast shade in the summer and can enliven the garden with showy flowers or fall color. For *instant* results, you can cover arbors with materials like shade cloth or lattice. But if you can be patient, the most permanent and elegant way to create shade is with trees.

SHADE TREES FOR SMALL SPACES

Choose trees carefully for the small shade garden; they will be the largest and most permanent feature. Many factors should influence tree selection. The canopy tree or trees in a small space should be small to medium-sized deciduous species that perform well in full sun and cast light-to-medium shade. (Most evergreens make dense cover, limiting the choice of plants that can grow underneath. In a small space, every inch counts!) Ideally, trees should have seasonal interest, such as mottled bark or showy fruit, and they should be pest and disease resistant and adapted to the conditions of your site.

Get a soil test done before making your selection; some trees need acid soil, and many urban areas have soils with a high pH (above 7) caused by alkaline construction rubble. All trees give other plants some competition for water and nutrients, but some are greedier than others, so avoid those with shallow roots. (See "Choosing Shade Trees," page 44). Also, be aware of the light needs of the plants you'll be growing under the tree: Most shade plants don't like heavy shade, and actually prefer light shade or high shade, especially if they're grown for their flowers, fruit or fall color.

Tree size and placement. Size and placement are critical, of course—especially in a small garden. Don't make the mistake of trying for an instant effect by planting too many trees or trees that will eventually grow to over 60 feet tall. To establish a shady area quickly, buy the largest trees appropriate for *continues on page 47*

Choose trees carefully for the small shade garden; they will be the largest and most permanent feature.

43

CHOOSING SHADE TREES

SOME TREES FOR ACID SOIL:

- Carolina silverbell, *Halesia tetraptera*
- Sourwood, *Oxydendrum arboreum*
- Serviceberry or Juneberry, *Amelanchier laevis, A. arborea, A. grandiflora*
- Sweetbay Magnolia, *Magnolia virginiana*

Serviceberry, Juneberry

Carolina Silverbell

Pawpaw

SOME TREES FOR ALKALINE SOIL:
- Golden-rain tree, *Koelreuteria paniculata*
- American smoketree, *Cotinus obovatus*

SOME pH ADAPTABLE TREES:
- Pawpaw, *Asimina triloba*
- Red buckeye, *Aesculus pavia*
- Horse chestnut, *Aesculus* x *carnea*
- Persian parrotia, *Parrotia persica*
- Paperbark maple, *Acer griseum*
- American hornbeam, *Carpinus caroliniana*

Paperbark Maple

TREES TO AVOID :
- Most evergreen trees (the shade they produce is too dense, and less rain reaches the soil surface)
- Deciduous trees that hold their branches close to the ground, such as Kousa dogwood (these are better used for larger spaces)
- Shallow-rooted trees like Norway and red maples, lindens and eastern white pine—choose deeper-rooted trees like yellowwood, cherries, crabapples and hawthorns

SUN- AND SHADE-ADAPTABLE PLANTS

Here are a few examples of plants that can adapt to both sun and shade:

Virginia Sweetspire

Woody plants—pawpaw, summersweet, nandina, winterberry, Virginia sweetspire, leatherleaf mahonia, witchhazel, Japanese maple, sweetshrub, winterhazel, holly osmanthus, viburnum, yew

Perennials—liriope, bugleweed, leadwort, yellow foxglove, clustered bell-flower, blue tube clematis, daylily, columbine, bergenia, Joe-pye weed, cardinal flower, blue star or amsonia, pink turtlehead, Japanese anemone, Japanese roof iris, bee balm, obedient plant

Bulbs—many, including daffodils, snowdrops, grape hyacinth, camassia, Guinea flower, siberian squill

Ornamental grasses—river oats

Hobblebush Viburnum

your space, but avoid overly large trees that will become out of scale with your property and will need to be removed much sooner than you would like them to be. Therefore, in a small space (say, 20 by 30 feet), you may want only one or two shade trees. You can plant trees 5 to 10 feet apart from center to center for an intimate feel, although I personally prefer the look that wider spacing provides. Small trees should be planted no closer to your house than 8 feet; even farther away is better. If you like a grove-like effect, a good solution in a small space may be to plant a multi-stemmed tree. My shade garden at home has a biodiverse tree collection (a politically correct way to be a collector!), but I intend to remove some trees when other trees start to get large enough.

Planting trees. If you choose the right tree or trees for your soil and climate, extensive soil preparation shouldn't be necessary (see "Gardening in the Shade," page 25). In urban areas with lots of construction debris, you may need to remove some of the existing soil and replace it with better soil. Tillage with a rototiller may be impossible; you may have to use a shovel and pickaxe or backhoe instead. Dump the existing soil in a compost pile if at all possible. Alternatively, you can construct raised beds to improve drainage and aeration.

Stimulate strong plant growth by watering adequately until the tree is established. If you choose to fertilize be careful not to overdo it: That can cause weak, floppy plant growth and excessive loss of nutrients by runoff or leaching.

SHRUBS FOR SHADE

Shrubs can also be used to create shade quickly. Some plants, such as red buckeye, Japanese spicebush and fringe tree, can be trained either as large shrubs or small trees. Other shrubs that can be used to create shade include rose-of-Sharon, spicebush, Chinese snowball and disanthus. If removing the lower limbs doesn't undermine the aesthetic appeal of the plant, many shrubs can be limbed up when they get large enough to allow shade-loving plants to be grown under them. Shade-loving plants can also be grown on the eastern and northern sides of shrubs. A drawback to using shrubs to create shade in a small space is that they may become too wide for the space and eventually may have to be removed.

OTHER PLANTS

The major challenge in converting a sunny area to a shade garden is using plants that can adapt as the area gets progressively shadier. The plants under and around trees will need to be sun tolerant until the tree canopy gets large enough.

The area under the tree canopy and the northern and eastern sides of trees will eventually have the most shade; this is also where you will be able to grow shade-loving plants first. Your best choices will be plants that are adaptable to both sun and shade (see box, page 46). You may want to grow hardy sun-loving plants in areas that eventually will be shady, then relocate them to a sunny area when your shade tree or trees have grown large. Another alternative, especially if you don't have sunny areas to move plants into, is to grow sun-loving annuals, biennials, and tender perennials in the areas that eventually will be shady.

Many shade-loving plants, such as most ferns and many perennials and woody plants, will not tolerate full sun—so plant these only after some shade is available. Some plants will tolerate full sun but may be plagued by insect and pest problems there, so it's better to wait until light shade is available before planting them (an example is evergreen azaleas, which often get damaged by lacebugs in full sun, at least in the Washington, D.C. area).

AN AESTHETICALLY PLEASING MIXTURE

Design considerations are also important when you're creating a woodland garden from scratch. A garden with a generous mixture of deciduous and evergreen shrubs, vines, groundcovers, bulbs, perennials, biennials, ferns, grasses and tender plants is stimulating and dynamic. This type of garden will maximize interest throughout the year and give your garden structure in the winter. Do exercise some restraint in plant selection, though, or the result will be a horticultural zoo with no cohesiveness. Each plant becomes more important in a small space because there will be fewer plants in the overall design. Resist the temptation to crowd plants together; use recommended spacings. To make your garden seem larger, use deep areas of planting to disguise property boundaries, or obscure some of the garden from view through careful placement of structures and shrubs.

In the shade garden the bulk of the bloom is in the springtime, so plants with attractive foliage and varying textures, shapes and forms are a must for interest in other seasons. For the greatest impact, group plants together that bloom at the same time. There are fewer shade-loving species that bloom in the summer and fall, and they generally have less showy flowers than sun-loving plants do. Plants with variegated leaves or golden leaves are one way to brighten up the shade garden in the summer and fall; another way is to grow colorful tender plants like caladium and nicotiana. And don't overlook the many other aspects of color that can also invigorate your shade garden, such as colorful fruit, seeds, bark and fall or winter interest.

A SUBURBAN WOODLAND GARDEN

Gardening Under Mature Lawn Trees

BY C. COLSTON BURRELL

LARGE TREES on older suburban lots provide sheltering shade and natural elegance—*and* pose a major challenge for gardeners. These open-grown trees usually have broad, dense crowns and shallow root systems. Because of the greedy tree roots, the soil under the trees is likely to be dry and not very fertile. Keeping a lawn going is seldom an option; under mature trees grass steadily declines, and continuing to reseed is futile. Sound like the ideal place to build a woodland garden? Maybe not ideal, but it may be your only choice—unless you *like* bare soil and patchy lawn. Why not give in? You already have the trees; all you need are organic matter, shrubs and shade-tolerant wildflowers.

Enriched soil in the cool shade of mature trees creates a perfect environment for a plethora of woodland plants.

Existing canopy trees form the ceiling of your garden room. Start planning the garden with the understory trees and shrubs, then move to the herbaceous plants. This duplicates the natural structure of the forest and maximizes the potential for supporting birds and other wildlife.

PLANNING YOUR GARDEN "ROOMS"

The existing canopy trees form the ceiling of the outdoor rooms of your new garden space. Exploit the open, root-free areas between the established trees wherever possible. Start planning the garden with the understory trees and shrubs, then move to the herbaceous plants. Understory trees bridge the gap between the canopy and the shrub layer, duplicating the natural structure of the forest and maximizing the potential for supporting birds and other wildlife. Small trees provide a sense of enclosure and a backdrop for the rest of the garden. Their flowers are always welcome in early spring: Spent petals shed across a garden path create an enchanting garden experience.

Think of shrubs as the walls of the garden rooms. Integrate them with the understory trees to form an edge of graduated heights that connects to the canopy. Use them to screen unattractive views such as the neighbors' trash cans, driveways and service areas. Shrubs are perfect for providing privacy; create secluded nooks and woodland hideaways with them. Shrubs can also help you manipulate your views. Try a mass planting at the curve of a path to veil the view and create a sense of mystery.

Once the architecture of the garden is in place, it's time for finishing touches. Wildflowers, bulbs and ferns are the real joy of woodland gardening. They form the colorful, textured carpet of the garden rooms.

PREPARING THE SOIL

To get started, first you need to get rid of the remaining grass. Even a struggling lawn will compete too much with your plants. If you go the non-chemical route—which is best for you and the environment—your options are either to strip the sod or to suffocate it. Stripping sod can be back-breaking work, and you need to be careful not to damage tree roots (especially on trees like oaks and sugar maples, which are sensitive to root disturbance). You can avoid wasting the topsoil and its associated microbes and help build organic matter by flipping the sod over and letting it decompose for about a month.

If you plan ahead, a less labor-intensive method is to smother the sod with a thick layer of mulch, but it does take up to three months before you can plant (see box). As a last resort, you can kill sod with a light application of the herbicide Roundup applied according to label directions. The grass will be dead and dry in 10 to 14 days. Next, cover the entire planting area with a 2- to 4-inch layer of compost or well-rotted manure.

Compost adds organic matter, which most lawns lack due to years of raking. Organic matter encourages earthworms and microbes, which re-establish healthy soil. It also increases the soil's porosity, nutrition and water-holding capacity as well. Enriched soil in the cool shade of mature trees creates a perfect environment for a plethora of woodland wildflowers and shrubs.

SMOTHERING SOD

To kill sod the easy and environmentally friendly way, smother it with newspaper and mulch. Start with several layers of newspaper, to form a covering about 1/2 to 1 inch thick (a single layer of corrugated cardboard will also work). Spread the paper evenly over the entire lawn area to be killed, and wet the paper thoroughly. Next, spread 2 to 4 inches of compost or mulch over the paper and water again. Leave the mulch in place for two to three months while the grass dies and decomposes. Once the sod is dead, you can plant right into the mulch.

TREES AND SHRUBS

Look next at the density and distribution of your trees. Too many trees make gardening a chore. If you have too many, choose what to cut with care. Remove fast-growing and weedy trees if possible. Silver maples are notorious for their difficult roots. Remove most maples, locust, mulberry and siberian elm before oaks, sugar maple and basswoods. Grind out the stumps and cart the shavings to the compost pile. Fill the stump hole with a mix of existing soil and compost.

It's often difficult to plant large shrubs under mature trees. Open-grown trees have shallow, woody roots that can be virtually impenetrable. Too much disturbance to the roots of sensitive trees may damage or kill them. To avoid problems, plant small trees and shrubs in the open, root-free zones between trees. If you must plant within the root zone of established trees, start with small, one-gallon shrubs or use bareroot stock whose roots can be manipulated to fit in odd-sized holes. Take care not to damage the bark of mature tree roots when you dig. When planting shrubs, trim rather than bend the roots to fit the hole. Bent roots will never straighten out and will eventually die; cut roots will quickly form lateral roots that aid in establishment. Top dress newly installed plants with 2 to 3 inches of organic matter. Keep plants well watered for an entire season to overcome the rigors of competition.

PLANTING AND MAINTAINING THE WOODLAND "CARPET"

Establishing and maintaining herbaceous plants under mature trees can also be a bugaboo. Open-grown lawn trees tend to have shallow, greedy roots that quickly garner all the water and nutrition, often to the detriment of the wildflowers. Give wildflowers a boost by enriching the soil before you plant. As with shrubs, take care when planting them under mature trees. Locate pockets of soil between large tree roots. Remove the existing soil and mix in generous amounts of compost. Put the enriched mixture back in the planting hole. Smooth the excess soil evenly over the root zone and top dress with a layer of organic matter.

To keep the soil healthy, provide an organic mulch each season. Trees produce a ready supply of leaves each autumn. Leave them in place to decay and slowly release nutrients. If you prefer a finer look, chopped leaves make an excellent summer mulch; the chopping can be done in autumn or in spring. If leaves are not available, top dress in the spring with a 1- to 2-inch layer of com-

Once the architecture of the garden is in place, it's time for the finishing touches. Wildflowers, bulbs and ferns are the real joy of woodland gardening. They form the colorful, textured carpet of the garden rooms.

post or well-rotted manure. Avoid coarse and woody mulches such as bark: They require vast amounts of nitrogen to decay, at the expense of your precious plants. With a proper mulching regime, weeds are seldom a problem once the garden is established. Tree seedlings may be prolific, though. Remove them while they're young and easy to pull. To reduce the need for irrigation, choose plants to match your existing conditions. Once plants are established, watering is seldom necessary. Over-watering may damage trees, especially oaks and other drought-tolerant species.

EDITING A MATURE WOODLAND
Shaping Change

BY SUSAN E. DUMAINE

CHANGE IS THE ESSENCE of a woodland garden. Gardening in the shade requires us to deal with this change and become nature's editor.

For more than 30 years, I've been editing a woodland in Zone 6A of New England, between granite ledges left behind by the last trans-Atlantic collision of tectonic plates. Shallow, acidic soils, usually rock packed but sometimes soft and floury, were deposited between these ledges by the glacial ice pack some ten thousand years ago. Until the early years of this century, this rough terrain served as the woodlot of a large farm in the adjacent glacial lake bed. Throughout New England, the end of small-scale agriculture has brought swift reforestation, and what we found on our two-acre property typifies the pattern of species distribution here. Although the species we encountered are particular to our region, the ongoing process we've employed in editing our woodland can be followed by gardeners across the country.

For more than 30 years the author has been trying to shape change in her woodland garden, shown here in May. But nature remains the senior editor.

EDITING THE CANOPY

The first step is observation. We started by taking inventory of the tree species on our site, noting the pattern of distribution as well as the effect of site conditions on growth habit. Back in 1961, we could see five mature, full crowned red oaks from the house. These stood in more open areas. Numerous younger red and white oaks dominated the ravine between the ledges. A few of the red oaks exhibited multiple trunks, evidence that they had once been cut. On the slopes, small groves of hemlock and beech occurred, with a few random examples of young hickory and red maple. Three chestnut sprouts alternately rose and fell to blight; one linden struggled to grow upright. A white pine was then and is now the tallest tree in the valley, progenitor of others that add feathery texture to the skyline. On and near the ledges in front of the house were two large white ash; in the valley, a few ash saplings.

Next comes editing out. In opening up the paths into and through the valley, my philosophy was to be as gentle with the existing canopy as possible, to exploit its virtues and to leave enough well-placed, well-shaped saplings for future canopy. I respected certain features of compelling interest—among them the existing groves and multi-trunked trees, as well as the hickories and oaks. I removed misshapen or redundant maples, beech and ash, which have shallower roots and are more difficult to garden beneath.

Over the years, nature has not entirely respected my philosophy, and remains the senior editor. Several majestic white oaks simply died, perhaps weakened by repeated gypsy moth defoliation. Five mature red oaks have succumbed to heart rot. Surprisingly, these dramatic, emotionally wrenching casualties have caused little obvious damage to other woody material. However, there has been a cost to the fabric of the woodland as a whole, for the meshing of both the canopy and root systems that once provided mutual support in high winds has been compromised.

When needed, we call in an arborist to remove broken branches in the canopy, or to limb up a tree to let in more light. Done in the winter, there is less debris and the cost is usually less. Done in the summer, it is possible to pinpoint what needs to be removed with great accuracy. On our property, as change admitted more light, saplings of ash and red maple grew strongly, and Norway maples, even faster growing, began to invade. I make yearly efforts to eradicate the weedy Norway maples, which are as fecund and undesirable as Norway rats, but the red maples are shapely and well placed. Ash decline, a newly recognized pestilence, is eliminating the ash one by one.

THE UNDERSTORY

In a woodland, understory trees and shrubs serve as visually important links between the canopy and herbaceous layers, helping to define spaces and create passages. Our understory had significant diversity, but was dominated by three distinct groves of arching white dogwood. Other dogwoods—pagoda, gray and blue—were also present. Three witchhazel spread their canopies on the south-facing slope, and in a seasonally wet area, two large spicebush brightened the early woodland with a veil of tiny sulphury flowers. Eight highbush blueberry grew in these moister spots as well, while lowbush blueberry scrambled over dry ledges. Here and there along the valley floor wandered the suckering, warty stems of elderberry. Maple-leaved viburnum grew over the rocky deposits in one end of the valley, pleasant with blue fall fruit and rosy leaves. In moist or dry spots, arrowwood rooted casually from supine branch tips. The blackhaw viburnum, more treelike, suckered into a thick grove, handsome in its fall fruit and foliage. A few young sassafras showed a similar tendency to grove.

Though the valley and its slopes were totally devoid of evergreen understory plants, there was a lot to respect and utilize. Each of the species we found remains somewhere in the garden, either because of its inherent interest or to reflect the habitat conditions. We have removed most of the arrowwood and sassafras, either because of poor form, poor flowering or simply excessive numbers. We also added the evergreens needed to give structure and year-round interest to the island compositions. We looked for variety in size, leaf form and texture in addition to flowers, and the evergreens now include hollies, rhododendrons, cherry laurels, andromeda, boxwood, laurel, yews, dwarf hemlocks, mahonia, leucothoe and viburnum. An unanticipated loss is the white flowering dogwood, which is declining in health and vigor all over the Northeast. In ten years, I have found neither the courage to completely remove it, nor anything to adequately replace it.

EDITING BY PRUNING

Editing by pruning is the key to maintaining the longterm vigor and aesthetic appeal of shrubs. This is true for evergreen woodlanders like carolina, catawba and rosebay rhododendrons as well as for deciduous shrubs like azaleas, viburnums or blueberry. At a minimum, some of the oldest stems need to be cut out regularly as the shrubs reach maturity. This encourages the development of young shoots and allows the shrubs to function as small trees, arching over path-

In a woodland garden where water is delivered as needed, an airy mulch maintained and the soil reworked from time to time, almost every plant will sooner or later seed about.

ways and framing views. If a truly fresh start is needed, they can usually be cut back to the ground, either just after flowering or in late winter. Either approach will direct the shrub's stored energy into the production of juvenile wood.

In a technique called arborizing, seriously overgrown, lanky rhododendrons and other shrubs can be pruned out so that their stems can be appreciated like tree trunks while their foliage encloses a space overhead. By emphasizing the vertical, many shrubs that have grown too wide for their location can be retained.

CURBING THE AGGRESSORS

Finally, you need to study the ground layer and decide what to keep, what to remove and what to add. Compared to the diversity of the woody material, the herbaceous flora in my woodland was depauperate, consisting of species able to tolerate considerable competition from roots and fallen leaves and endure our typically dry summers without supplemental water. Evergreen whorls of marginal shield fern hung from crevices in the ledges. Elsewhere, stoloniferous asters, sarsaparilla, wild oats, hay-scented fern and false Solomon's-seal, aggressors all, covered large sweeps. I still allow them generous space, but stand ready to smother them with mulch-topped strips of old carpet when necessary.

When needed, an arborist is called in to remove broken branches in the canopy.

Some of the plants I introduced in making the garden have been overly successful, and I have had to cope with their excess. Plants set out for quick cover—such as golden archangel and even my favorite evergreen groundcover, creeping phlox—do just that, and then don't know how to stop. Grouped for texture, groundcovers such as barren strawberry, foamflower and ginger eventually run into each other, and need to be separated and replanted. Charmers such as celandine poppy and wild bleeding heart, which delight us with their extended flowering period, overwhelm with their numbers in time.

In a woodland garden where water is delivered as needed, an airy mulch maintained and the soil reworked from time to time, almost every plant, from meadow rues to bugbanes, will sooner or later seed about. Before too long, editing becomes central to the garden's maintenance, and the best red pen is a fearlessly used compost pile.

A DRY WOODLAND GARDEN
Coping with Dry Shade

BY MARY ELLEN TONSING

WHEN WE THINK OF A WOODLAND GARDEN, most of us envision a cool, moist, lush oasis. If you live in a dry climate, though, creating that vision is more of a challenge.

Where I garden, in the plains east of the Rocky Mountains, there is less annual rainfall than on either coastal area. Long periods of hot, dry weather and low humidity dry out the soil. Winters bring warm, sunny days with cold nights. This constant freezing and thawing causes plants to heave out of the soil, exposing roots. The property I garden on is an acre edged at its borders with large, old deciduous trees, including a straight line of very tall Colorado spruce trees that divides the property in half. Trees create areas of light shade, filtered shade, deep shade and dry shade. The trees are shallow rooted, so they rob the soil of nutrients and water.

For years I didn't know how to deal with such conditions. Our house and driveway are on one half of the property, and the other half was planted with grass that made a perfect "park" for my children and all of the neighborhood children. Once the children were grown and not having daily football or baseball games, we built a Victorian gazebo right in the middle of the "park" and put in a shade border.

CHOOSING DROUGHT-TOLERANT PLANTS

The first rule in dealing with dry shade and other extreme weather conditions is to choose appropriate plants, including natives that have adapted to these conditions. Plants use water less efficiently at the higher altitudes where I garden, so it's especially important to grow drought-tolerant plants.

Before settlers arrived carrying shade trees in their covered wagons along with their household goods, the plains east of the Rocky Mountains were home to drought-tolerant, sun-loving plants. We have no native woodlands or shade-loving wildflowers here. The native wildflowers that prefer shade grow along the stream banks in the mountains and need pampering to survive on the plains. But adventurous gardeners have tested plants from other areas of the country to see if they would adapt to our growing conditions. Creeping holly berry (*Mahonia repens)* makes a good groundcover for difficult areas. It has year-round interest, with holly-like evergreen leaves, yellow flowers in the spring and black-purple fruits in the fall. Periwinkle is another good evergreen groundcover, with pretty blue flowers in the spring. Coral bells are popular border plants because they flower for such a long time in the summer. Small red, white or pink flowers form along the edge of thin, wiry stems; the attractive basal leaves are evergreen. One of the prettiest spring bloomers is perennial forget-me-not, with its dark green, heart-shaped leaves and bright blue flowers that complement spring bulbs.

While water-wise plantings are encouraged, supplemental watering of trees

In a dry climate it's best to use moisture-loving shade plantings sparingly and in a limited area, to cut down on the need for supplemental watering.

and shrubs is necessary during long, dry periods. Many gardeners in the Rocky Mountain region develop an interest in primulas, cyclamen, epimediums or, in my case, ferns. It's just best to use the moisture-loving plantings sparingly and in a limited area, to cut down on the need for watering.

PREPARING THE SOIL

After deciding on the shape and size of our shade border, I began preparing the soil. Eighty years ago, when our house was built, our property was part of an old farm. Consequently, our top soil was never removed as is the practice today in new housing developments. The soil had been amended by previous owners through the years, so we started with a good base. It's only when I start digging deeper that I run into alkaline clay soil. There are many plants that grow well in this type of soil, including Rocky Mountain columbine, European wild ginger, pussytoes, hostas, barrenwort, kinnikinick and the Lenten rose.

Good soil preparation is the key to successful shade gardening in a semi-arid region. The work is hard and time consuming but well worth the effort. If you're planning a garden in clay soil with little annual rainfall and strong winds, you have to add organic matter to the soil to loosen and aerate it. Compost is a great additive; it makes the soil lighter, allowing more air and water to get to the roots. Shredded leaves or leaf mold are also good additives. It takes several years to build a good, humus-rich soil, depending upon the original condition of the soil. A top-dressing of organic mulch or compost every spring, along with mulching every fall with shredded leaves, continuously builds the soil. Each spring as I add new plants, I amend the soil before planting.

MULCHING AND WATERING

Another way to retain moisture in the soil is by mulching. The annual leaf drop in natural woodlands produces a rich, deep mulch. Whether in a native woodland or the garden, mulches reduce evaporation, improve water penetration and regulate soil temperature. Organic mulches decompose over a period of time and improve the soil. Also, a crust doesn't form on top of the soil, so the water infiltrates freely. Compost, shredded leaves, small bark or wood chips and even groundcovers all make good mulches. Many plants prefer the cool root run that heavy mulching provides. Mulching also helps to protect the roots exposed by alternate freezing and thawing.

Because I also grow many acid-loving plants, I mulch every spring with

Mulch helps retain soil moisture, reduce evaporation, improve water penetration and regulate soil temperature. Many plants prefer the cool root run that heavy mulching provides. Mulching also helps to protect the roots exposed by alternate freezing and thawing.

shredded pine needles, which are very acidic. As the needles break down during the year they help to neutralize the pH of our naturally alkaline soil.

Because of our low annual rainfall, under 15 inches, supplemental watering during the growing season is necessary—not only for the vegetables and perennials, but for trees and shrubs as well. We also often have to water once or twice during the dry winter months.

To avoid wasting this natural resource, it's important to keep watering to a minimum and to find the most efficient method. Check your soil before watering to see if it really is needed. Don't water during the heat of the day. Drip irrigation or soaker hoses work better in borders than overhead watering where the evaporation rate is greater. Trying to water overhead on a windy day is futile and wasteful. One advantage of gardening in a dry climate: We rarely worry about rot or molds.

Gardening in Dense, Year-round Shade

BY DANIEL J. HINKLEY

THROUGHOUT MUCH OF NORTH AMERICA, woodland gardening can present perplexing challenges and munificent rewards to the horticultural enthusiast. The rewards are no less to those of us gardening in the dense, year-round shade of conifers—although our efforts are met by a specific assemblage of hurdles.

Gardening under conifers in the Pacific Northwest, for example, means coaxing plants through cool summers that are normally painfully dry. Occasional misty showers serve only to moisten the needled branches of our common overstory species—Douglas firs, western red cedars and western hemlocks—and rarely reach the ground. These large coniferous trees themselves accentuate the problem, pilfering any hydraulic surplus from the topsoil very early in the growing season.

Converting the conifer woodland to garden is not an exceptionally difficult task, however. By following basic guidelines of soil preparation and plant selection, you can create a woodland garden of quiet charm or exuberant color with appeal that spans the seasons.

TAKING INVENTORY

Start by taking a hard look at the plant inventory already on the site. Often, hidden within a rampant understory of brambles, elderberry and nettles, are handsome native plants. With selective, rather than wholesale, clearing of the site you can preserve these specimens, making the additional effort worthwhile.

In the cool, dry summers of the Pacific Northwest, occasional misty showers serve mostly to dampen the needled branches of the overstory trees.

The low-elevation coniferous woodlands of the Pacific Northwest are particularly easy to decipher, due to the relative paucity of native species. Below the overstory of conifers, we may find a few understory trees, including vine maple and western dogwood—both of which are ornamental components of our ecology. We may also find shrubs, including salal, red huckleberry, evergreen huckleberry and the bigleaf rhododendron. Interspersed are an assortment of brambles, ferns and groundcovers that may be either a cherished component or formidable foe to the gardener.

As in woodlands across the globe, most plant activity here occurs in early to midspring when there remains an excess of available soil moisture from our winter rains. Fresh spring growth and flowers of April and May give way to quiet greens and russets as many herbaceous plants slip into midsummer dormancy. If adequate light is available, autumn brings dashes of bright goldens and reds from our native maples, elderberry and Indian plum, although it's a rather sleepy performance compared to the autumnal blaze of hardwood forests in eastern North America.

Once the plant palette is edited to your liking, defining the space with bed shapes and a trail system will not only afford readier access for maintenance and enjoyment, but also will allow more thoughtful placement of diminutive treasures where they can be easily enjoyed. Many choice woodland species thrive under our conditions. Witchhazel and sweet box will often be in full blossom by Christmas, soon followed by a large collection of hellebores. In early February, the chartreuse flowers of *Helleborus viridis* ssp. *viridis* blossom in concert with the intense blues of blue corydalis. Many trillium species begin to emerge from the ground as early as mid-February, producing a diverse and colorful floral display for several weeks. A little later, *Pulmonaria* species and cultivars carpet the floor of the garden, providing bespeckled foliage and a wide range of color from an early and long-flowering display. They are followed by the early *Arisaema* species, whose intriguing, hooded flowers are enjoyed in combination with dramatic foliage and mottled stems. Early summer brings the blossoms of hydrangeas and *Cardiocrinum giganteum,* a monocarpic lily from China and the Himalaya that soars to 15 feet, capped with up to 20 enormous lilies that fill the entire garden with their fragrance.

In our own woodland, we have designed a circuitous system of paths throughout by lowering the trail by 8 to 10 inches in relation to the planting beds. This keeps visitors to the garden on the paths, provides a sense of elevational change, creates a more intimate association with the plants and provides greater ease in maintenance. Over time, the trail has filled with falling needles from the overstory of Douglas firs, creating a quiet carpet.

PREPARING THE SOIL

The dry, acidic soil under conifers requires special preparation. Organic matter, such as manure, compost or even fine bark, will greatly improve the tilth and water-holding capacity of the soil. A minimum of 4 inches of your chosen amendment should be blended into the top foot of soil. Incorporating a complete fertilizer will aid in plant establishment. Remember to use a higher-nitrogen fertilizer— at a rate of 1 pound of nitrogen per 1,000 square feet—if you have used sawdust or bark for your organic matter, since they rob this nutrient from the soil. Organic fertilizers such as milorganite do a good job. Due to our heavy rainfalls, the soils of western Washington are particularly infertile; we are especially shy in nitrogen and phosphorus. Supplemental feeding at planting helps insure establishment. As plants mature, though, they probably won't need such help unless they show signs of deficiency.

CHOOSING APPROPRIATE PLANTS

Selecting plants to include in your garden is certainly the most exciting aspect of the venture. It's helpful to approach this task in a well organized manner, and it's critical to select plants that will do well in the dry, year-round shade of conifers.

Understory trees. Begin by selecting a few understory trees, either evergreen or deciduous, to "lower" the ceiling of your garden and create a more intimate feel. The striped-bark maples are exceptional choices for this role. Their bold foliage provides additional shade during the growing season, while their white-striped skeletal framework adds interest to the garden during the months of dormancy. *Stewartia pseudocamellia* and *S. monadelpha* perform admirably in light shade, providing silken spring blossoms of white, good autumn coloration and striking mottled winter bark. Golden-foliaged trees such as *Robinia pseudoacacia* 'Frisia' shine in our woodland with brilliant chartreuse foliage throughout summer. Although this tree will grow in full sun, many golden or variegated-foliaged trees and shrubs require protection from full sun in order to prevent leaf scorch. I also grow flowering apricot in my woodland to protect it from late winter freezes that might damage the flower buds. Although it blooms noticeably later because of the siting, it blossoms quite freely and fills the garden with its heavy, fruity fragrance.

Shrubs. Next, choose shrubs adapted to shady conditions to connect the understory and the forest floor. There are many deciduous and evergreen shrubs to use in our woodlands. The deciduous shrubs add a lively exchange to the spring garden as their bright green foliage emerges, while their evergreen counterparts remain in foliage to carry the garden through the off season. For deciduous shrubs consider *Eleutherococcus sieboldianus* 'Variegatus', with five-fingered leaves, each neatly margined in white; Virginia sweetspire, which produces midsummer nodding white racemes and handsome red autumn color, and *Rubus* 'Benenden' (*R.* x *tridel*), a hybrid bramble with enormous single white flowers along 6-foot-long thornless arching canes. Evergreen shrubs that do well include the many species of winter box, which blossoms in the depths of winter with incomparable fragrance, and Japanese aucuba in its many forms, with broad evergreen leaves and good crops of red fruit on female plants. Both sexes of Japanese skimmia are exceptional—the males for their large heads of fragrant flowers and the females for a crop of red fruit that is held throughout winter. Mahonia species and hybrids have handsome, glossy pinnate foliage and produce heads of yellow flowers in winter or early spring.

With the proper soil preparation and plant selection, you can create a conifer woodland garden of quiet charm or exuberant color with appeal that spans the seasons.

Groundcovers and perennials. Finally, lay the "carpet" of groundcovers and herbaceous woodland plants. Goundcovers may include the imperturbable *Euphorbia amygdaloides* var. *robbiae* (Miss Robb's Spurge), with its evergreen foliage and bright chartreuse flowers in early spring; foamflower, with semi-evergreen leaves and candle-like white flowers in April and May; *Rubus pentalobus* and *Rubus tricolor,* with their vigorously spreading stems cloaked by unblemished evergreen leaves; and evergreen *Vancouveria,* with its glossy foliage and airy white sprays of flowers in May and June. Take care during this step to avoid siting vigorous groundcovers adjacent to more fragile ones. Pachysandra, for example, will quickly swamp trilliums or gentians, rendering them too weak to blossom over time. Consider reserving one bed simply for the less pushy, clumping perennials, and plant the others entirely with romping, weed-smothering groundcovers.

67

TURNING A FOREST INTO A GARDEN
"Enhancing" a Native Woodland

BY WAYNE WOMACK

THE VERY ACT of buying a woodland property suggests that old desire to return to nature. Two important things that you discover much later are 1) your ego begins to give way to the vagaries of nature and 2) you become less bent on taming and controlling the landscape that you so blithely entered.

This was certainly true of the one-acre woodland in Baton Rouge, Louisiana, where our home is located. In the deep South the impact of a woodland can be powerful, with enclosures of mature trees soaring at times over 100 feet and suggesting a cathedral-like atmosphere. Woodlands here have dense tree spacing and undergrowth. We dreamed of an overstory of oak and hickory, but our woodland was covered with sweet gum with an oversupply of gum balls and no significant fall foliage color.

Nonetheless, we set out to turn our tangled forest into a woodland *garden*. The steps we took can be followed in similar situations in any region and climate.

FINDING THE OPEN AREAS

The first step is to clear the underbrush. On our property, air circulation was poor and mosquitos were a constant menace, so we began by clearing the underbrush, where elderberry, briars and honeysuckle were prevalent. Once able to move freely among the trees, we could determine where the most open areas were located. The idea was to create a sequence of spaces that would allow sunlight in—both for contrast with the shaded areas and to provide for plants that require higher light levels. In all, we removed some 80 trees, 6-inch caliper or less, which left the larger trees spaced 10 to 20 feet apart. This distribution provided room for the crowns to develop, while keeping the rhythm of the tree trunks.

OBSERVING THE NATIVE LANDSCAPE

Once the first clearing is done, the real design can begin. One delight of making a woodland garden is the opportunity to design a vertical layering of differing-height trees and shrubs that can fit comfortably together. The best approach in developing a design for your woodland garden is to carefully observe the character of the native woodland. That way even if you use non-native plants, you can still echo the native landscape. You can also pick up clues about the habit, spacing and arrangement of plants.

When analyzing plants in design terms we inevitably think of three main qualities: the form and structure of a plant, the texture of its foliage and the seasonal color of flowers, fruit and leaves. In the deep South plants grow rampantly as the result of a mild and lengthy growing season with frequent rainfall. The native woods can appear visually chaotic in terms of form. The rich tangle of vines, sprawling herbaceous plants and shrubs and trees is seldom regular and tidy. It can seem so overwhelming that the natural reaction is to exert control and simplify. There is also unpredictability in native woods; it's best to learn to enjoy this unpredictability in your own garden as well.

Carefully observe the character of native woodlands. That way, even if you use non-native plants you can still echo the local landscape structure.

Texture is important in any woodland, and it seems the most comprehensible aspect of the native southern woodland. Various leaf sizes and shapes, both deciduous and evergreen, mingle to create a highly sensual tapestry. A variety of broadleaf evergreens creates a unique effect. Color through the seasons is subtle, with green always seemingly dominant. Native woodland flowers are usually small and tend to pastels of yellow and white. Blue is rare, and dulled purples and reds are found in relatively small flowers. Spring is rich and varied with many flowers and an amazing range of green foliage. Summer is lush and dense. Fall foliage color is unpredictable, but there is a compensatory variety of flowers and fruit. Winter is exhilarating with its berries and evergreens revealed in a bright, warm light.

CHOOSING PLANTS

In our case, we did not want so much to recreate the native woodland as to create our own "enhanced" version of it. The woods here can seem exotic, with coarse textures and a general density of effect. We used tropical plants such as gingers, crinums and curcumas to enhance the lushness. Lustrous evergreens such as viburnums and camellias reflect light and add sparkle in the heavy summer shade. The native woods have subtle fragrances throughout the year, and therefore winter honeysuckle, gardenia and banana shrub are good choices.

You can choose plants to lighten the ground plane of the garden, too. Plants with gray and white variegated leaves, such as varieties of pittosporum, cleyera, aspidistra and liriope, give our garden a playfulness and an element of surprise. Because of the dominance of the tall trees and the way they pull the eye upward, we decided to use a rich variety of low shrubs and herbaceous plants to draw attention to the ground plane. We are great lovers of ferns and decided to use their fine textures over much of the garden to make the horizontal plane of the ground seem larger. Coarse-textured plants push up through them as accents.

ADDING THE "UNKNOWN"

Next, try to add some unpredictability. The joy of a walk through the native woods is the anticipation of the unknown—that sense of wondering on each trip what you will find. We have tried to bring that quality to our garden. The stepping stone paths through the garden were added some ten years after the plant-

The southern woodland is dense and exotic looking, with coarse textures. The author uses hardy tropical ferns and curcumas to enhance the lushness.

ings; the revelations of maturing plants determined where the walks would be located. There are dead-end walks where you are greeted with a surprise (in one case a gray-flowered Louisiana iris clump), before returning to the main path. Plants should seem unpredictable in their location. So often a rare or showy plant is located in a conspicuous place. It can be more interesting to take a spectacular plant such as a bigleaf magnolia or a crinum and place it where it's less obvious. If this approach seems quirky, consider that the experience of roaming a woodland is much the same—spontaneous, unpredictable and seemingly random.

The garden in spring. Color in the native southern woodland is subtle, with green always dominant.

MAINTENANCE

There is always the great shadow of maintenance hovering over a garden. We have learned to allow ours to be "untidy" just as a wild woodland—not swept clean and every twig picked up. If cleanup is important, winter is the best time here as the weather is mild. Winter is a favorite season for us. The plants seem relaxed, and many interesting odors scent the air. During the growing season it is fascinating to watch plants move of their own volition to different locations. A colony of trillium or ardisia or a seedling mahonia might appear in an unexpected place. You begin to realize that the garden is asserting its independence—the sign of a healthy garden. Once you have planted your woodland garden with thought and inspiration, sit back and let it become what it will. That's when the rewards begin.

WOODLAND PLANTS

The scores of spectacular woodland plants—trees, shrubs, wildflowers and ferns—featured in the pages that follow can form the foundation of a delightful woodland garden. The plants are organized by region. If you are interested in restoring local plant communities, note that some of the featured plants for each region are native to that particular area of the country and are listed separately from those indigenous to other regions of the United States or to other countries.

THE MID-ATLANTIC
ZONES 5 TO 8

The climate of the Mid-Atlantic, from the Adirondacks through southeastern coastal Virginia, is temperate. Annual minimum temperatures range widely, with temperatures dropping below 0°F in most of the region at some point during the winter. Snow cover is not reliable. Summers are hot and humid, with temperatures commonly reaching into the high 90s. It is somewhat cooler in the mountains than in the Piedmont and coastal plain. Mineral soils are usually moderately acid, although soils influenced by limestone bedrock in many mountain valleys are pH neutral. Soils have low to moderate levels of organic matter; silt loams and sandy loams are predominant, but in many areas the original topsoil has been removed by erosion or development, and clay subsoils are often what remains.

15 GREAT WOODLAND PLANTS FOR THE MID-ATLANTIC

NATIVE:

Shuttleworth's Ginger
Asarum shuttleworthii
Evergreen groundcover 6" tall; spreads slowly. Rounded foliage with elegant light green to silvery white mottling. Large, solitary flowers are brownish and hidden by foliage. *A. canadense*, wild ginger, is deciduous; *A. arifolium*, *A. minus* and *A. virginicum* are evergreen natives. Plant in rich, acid soil in light to partial shade. Zones 4 to 9.

Black Snakeroot or Black Cohosh
Cimicifuga racemosa
Deciduous perennial; 3' to 8' tall when flowering in midsummer. Attractive, large, compound leaves. Flowers are long, white, wand-like spires; spent flower spires are decorative for many weeks. Plant in humus-rich, moist soil in light to partial shade. Gypsum can be added to the soil at planting time to increase calcium uptake; fertilize light-

Foamflower

Virginia Bluebells

ple. Clusters of white, pitcher-shaped flowers in May are somewhat hidden by the foliage. Grow in light to full shade. Prefers moist, acidic, well-drained soil with lots of organic matter; drought tolerant when established. Zones 6 to 9.

Virginia Bluebells
Mertensia virginica
1'- to 2'-tall perennial that is a spring ephemeral (summer dormant) with a fleshy rootstock. In early spring, pinkish buds open into splendid trumpet-shaped, nodding sky-blue flowers. Large, rounded leaves are medium green until they die down in June. Grow in light to partial shade in rich, moist soil. Exquisite in mass along streams and under spring-blooming trees such as magnolias. Plant with non-ephemerals such as wild ginger or ferns. Zones 3 to 8.

Foamflower
Tiarella cordifolia
Impressive evergreen groundcover, 6" to 12" tall. Charming in bloom, with spires of white or light pink blossoms in midspring. Usually spreads by stolons. Attractive foliage is broadly lobed, and in some cultivars deeply cut; often dusted with red or purple markings. Foliage often has an ornamental bronze or burgundy color during the winter. Grow in light to partial shade in well-drained, moist, rich, acid soil. Zones 3 to 8.

ly in the spring. No staking needed. Zones 3 to 8.

Dwarf Crested Iris
Iris cristata
6"- to 10"-tall deciduous perennial; an excellent groundcover and foliage plant. Creeping rhizomes send up linear iris foliage. Delightful flowers just above the foliage in midspring—usually pale blue, but also white, lavender, dark blue or violet. Grow in well-drained, rich soil in light to partial shade. Do not cover the top of the rhizomes with mulch. Zones 4 to 8.

Drooping Leucothoe
Leucothoë fontanesiana
Small evergreen shrub, from 3' to 6' tall and wide. Arching branches with long, pointed leaves that are dark green at maturity, with an overall fountain-like effect. Winter foliage color varies from bronze to rich pur-

Yellowroot
Xanthorhiza simplicissima
Deciduous dwarf shrub or tall groundcover 2' to 3' tall. Attractive, celery-like
leaves on erect stems. Fall color is yellow to red or purple. Interesting pur-
ple-brown flowers in drooping clusters
appear before the leaves unfold. Wonderful foliage plant in light to full
shade in wet to moist, acidic soils.
Zones 3 to 9.

Lenten Rose

NON-NATIVE:

Yellow-flowered Barrenwort
Epimedium x *versicolor* 'Sulphureum'
Enchanting, tough deciduous perennial, about 1' tall. Yellow flowers with
spurs in airy sprays in early spring.
Compound foliage with heart-shaped
leaflets. Grow in light to full shade in
soil rich in organic matter. Tolerates
dry soil, but does best in moist soil.
Clip spent foliage to the ground in late
winter. Spreads by rhizomes. Zones 4
to 8.

Lenten Rose
Helleborus orientalis (*H.* x *hybridus*)
Evergreen perennial, 18" to 24" tall. A
long winter/spring bloom. Nodding,
cup-shaped flowers range from pale
green, white or pink to maroon with
showy golden stamens, often with
speckling inside. Foliage is glossy,
leathery and deeply cut. Grow in light
to partial shade in moist, rich soil.
Zones 4 to 8.

Japanese Spicebush
Lindera obtusiloba
10'- to 20'-tall deciduous shrub or small
tree. Small yellow flowers in early spring
are somewhat larger than the native *L.
benzoin*. Stunning yellow fall foliage.
Black fruits on female plants. Prefers
moist sites in light to partial shade.
Zones 6 to 9.

Variegated Japanese Solomon's-seal
Polygonatum odoratum 'Variegatum'
Deciduous perennial, 18" to 24" tall.
Marvelous arching foliage; leaves
edged with white. Spreads by rhi-
zomes. Clusters of greenish-white

Variegated Japanese Solomon's-seal

flowers dangle from underneath the leaves in mid-spring. Greenish-black fruit and soft yellow foliage in fall. *P. biflorum* is native. Light to partial shade in moist, rich soil. Zones 3 to 8.

Japanese Tassel Fern
Polystichum polyblepharum
Choice evergreen fern, 1' to 2' tall with lustrous, dark green fronds. Emerging fronds are tassel-like. Stipe and rachis (the stems in ferns) are heavily covered with brown scales, adding interest. Vase-shaped habit. *P. acrostichoides*, Christmas Fern, is native. Grow in light to full shade in acidic, humus-rich soil. Zones 4 to 9.

Sacred Lily of China
Rohdea japonica
Evergreen perennial with unique wide, dark green, leathery foliage up to 2' long. Rosette of leaves grows 9" to 15" tall, making it an excellent groundcover. Pale yellow flowers are hidden by the foliage. Fat red berries from mid fall through winter. Grow in light to full shade in soil enriched with organic matter. Zones 6 to 9.

Moonlight Japanese Hydrangea vine
Schizophragma hydrangeoides 'Moonlight'
Deciduous woody vine with handsome silver mottling on heart-shaped leaves. Eventually grows 25' tall. Clinging vine with lacy heads of white, slightly nodding, hydrangea-like flowers in early

summer. Gold fall color. Grow in light to partial shade in rich, moist, well-drained soil. Zones 5 to 8.

Japanese Tassel Fern

Toadlily
Tricyrtis hirta
Deciduous 2'- to 3'-tall perennial with small, jewel-like flowers in the fall. Stems can be gracefully arching or more upright. Foliage color is usually medium green. Cultivars and hybrids superior to the species: 'Kohaku' has larger white flowers with purple spotting and yellow throat; 'Sinonome' has white flowers heavily speckled with purple; 'Variegata' has white flowers speckled with purple, with slender cream margin on leaves. Grow in light to partial shade in moist soil with abundant organic matter. Place near the edge of beds so that people can enjoy the flowers as they walk by. Zones 4 to 8.

MORE WOODLAND PLANTS FOR THE MID-ATLANTIC

TREES:

Asimina triloba, Pawpaw
Magnolia fraseri, Fraser Magnolia
M. tripetala, Umbrella Magnolia

SHRUBS AND VINES:

Aesculus parviflora, Bottlebrush Buckeye
Cephalotaxus harringtonia 'Prostrata', 'Duke Gardens', Japanese Plum Yew
Clethra acuminata, Cinnamon Clethra
C. alnifolia, Summersweet
Corylopsis pauciflora, Buttercup Winterhazel
Fothergilla gardenii, F. major—Fothergilla
Hamamelis x *intermedia*, Witchhazel
Hedera colchica 'Sulfur Heart', Colchis Ivy
Hydrangea quercifolia, Oakleaf Hydrangea
Ilex verticillata 'Winter Red' and the hybrid 'Sparkleberry', Winterberry Holly
Itea virginica, Virginia Sweetspire
Kalmia latifolia and cultivars, Mountain Laurel
Lindera benzoin, Spicebush
Mahonia bealei, Leatherleaf Mahonia
M. japonica, Japanese Mahonia
Nandina domestica 'Harbor Dwarf', 'Moon Bay', Nandina
Parthenocissus henryana, Silvervein Virginia Creeper
Rhododendron species and hybrids, Azaleas and Rhododendrons
Thujopsis dolobrata 'Nana', Dwarf False Arborvitae
Viburnum nudum 'Winterthur', Viburnum

PERENNIALS:

Actaea pachypoda (A. alba), Doll's Eyes
Ajuga reptans, Bugleweed
Anemone x *hybrida*, Flowering Anemone
Aralia racemosa, Spikenard
Arum italicum 'Pictum' and 'Dr. Comstock', Italian Arum
Aruncus dioicus, Goatsbeard

Aster divaricatus, White Wood Aster
Astilbe x *arendsii* cultivars, Astilbe
Begonia grandis, Hardy Begonia
Chelone obliqua, Pink Turtlehead
Dicentra eximia, Wild Bleeding Heart
Galanthus nivalis, Snowdrops
Geranium x 'Johnson's Blue', Cranesbill
G. maculatum, Wild Geranium
Heuchera americana 'Garnet', 'Dale's Strain' and hybrids 'Pewter Veil', 'Ruby Veil', Alumroot
Hosta species and cultivars
Liriope muscari, Blue Lily-turf
Lobelia cardinalis and cultivars, Cardinal Flower
Mitchella repens, Partridgeberry
Narcissus hybrids, Daffodil
Pachysandra procumbens, Alleghany Pachysandra
Phlox stolonifera 'Bruce's White', 'Sherwood Purple', Creeping Phlox
P. divaricata, Wild Blue Phlox
Pulmonaria saccharata 'Roy Davidson' and *P.* 'Excalibur', Lungwort
Sanguinaria canadensis, Bloodroot
Smilacina racemosa and *S. stellata*, False Solomon's-seal
Stylophorum diphyllum, Yellow Wood Poppy
Thalictrum rochebrunianum, Meadow Rue
Vancouveria hexandra, Inside-out Flower
Vinca minor, Periwinkle

GRASSES AND GRASSLIKE PLANTS:

Carex plantaginea, C. siderosticta 'Variegata', *C. grayi*, Plantain-like Sedge
Chasmanthium latifolium, River Oats
Hakonechloa macra 'Aureola', Variegated Hakone Grass
Luzula nivea, Snowy Woodrush

FERNS:

Adiantum pedatum, Maidenhair Fern
Athyrium species, including *A. nipponicum* 'Pictum', Japanese Painted Fern, *A. otophorum* and *A filix-femina*
Dryopteris species, including *D. erythrosora, D. goldiana, D. ludoviciana*, Wood Fern

THE UPPER MIDWEST
ZONES 3 TO 5

Temperatures in the Upper Midwest are marked by extremes: The winter temperature can drop below -30°F for weeks on end, and summer temperatures may soar to the mid 90s. The vagaries of climate severely limit woody vegetation, but the generally persistent snow cover gives great leeway with perennial plants, especially in Zones 3 and 4. The mineral soils are rich clay or silt loams with a mantle of organic soil. Many of the soils are influenced by limestone bedrock and are slightly acidic to slightly alkaline. In some areas, alkaline clay poses unique gardening challenges.

15 GREAT WOODLAND PLANTS FOR THE UPPER MIDWEST

NATIVE:

Maidenhair
Adiantum pedatum
Elegant, deciduous fern with 2'-tall horseshoe-shaped fronds sporting slender, finger-like divisions. Ebony stems and pink fiddleheads decorative in spring. Forms thick clumps. Prefers deep, humus-rich, moist soil in light to full shade. Established plants tolerate drought by going dormant. Zones 3 to 8.

Spikenard
Aralia racemosa
Graceful, shrubby plant 3' to 5' tall with a 3' spread. Huge, divided leaves lend a tropical air to northern gardens. Dense, tiered clusters of green flowers are followed by showy purple berries. Prefers humus-rich soil in light to deep shade. Perfect as a backdrop to delicate flowers and ferns. Thrives under evergreens. In warmer areas, plants go dormant in late summer. Zones 3 to 8.

Pagoda Dogwood
Cornus alternifolia
A refined understory tree 30' or taller. Horizontal tiered branches. Flattened clusters of small, creamy-white flowers above the foliage in late spring and

Maidenhair Fern

early summer. Showy blue-black fruits on red pedicels follow in the late summer. Leaves yellow in autumn. Prefers moist, neutral to slightly acidic, humus-rich soil in light to partial shade. Zones 3 to 8.

Twinleaf
Jeffersonia diphylla
Delicate white flowers open with the leaves and shatter in a few days with wind and rain. Decorative leaves resemble butterflies. Clumps grow 1' high from slow-creeping, fibrous-rooted crowns. Plant in moist, neutral soil in light to full shade. Combine with wildflowers and ferns or use as a coarse groundcover under large shrubs and flowering trees. Zones 3 to 7.

Blue Phlox
Phlox divaricata
Perfumed clusters of sky-blue flowers

Blue Phlox

top 1' stems in early to mid spring. Plants form a low, evergreen carpet from creeping, fibrous-rooted stems. Plant in moist, neutral soil in light to full shade. Many cultivars available in shades from white to purple. Zones 3 to 8.

Zig-zag Goldenrod
Solidago flexicaulis
Woodland goldenrods are excellent for late season color in the shade. Plants grow 2' to 2-1/2' tall from fibrous-rooted crowns. Oval, toothed leaves alternate up crooked stems. Flowers are clustered in the leaf axils. Grow in moist, neutral to acidic, humus-rich soil in sun or shade. Zones 3 to 8.

Maple-leaf Viburnum
Viburnum acerifolium
Enchanting 4'- to 6'-tall shrub with an arching, open habit. Leaves resemble a maple; flowers are creamy-white in mounded clusters in late spring.

Twinleaf

Black-purple berries follow in late summer. Autumn color is dusty-rose. Grow in moist to dry, acidic, humus-rich soil in sun or shade; tolerates deep shade. Zones 3 to 8.

Himalayan Maidenhair
Adiantum venustum
This delicate fern adds a tropical air to the garden. The 6" to 12" fronds are intricately divided into small, wedge-shaped leaflets. Forms dense, ever-green clumps. Grow in moist, neutral to acidic, humus-rich soil in light to full shade. Perfect as a groundcover under shrubs. Succeeds well in colder zones where the similar southern maidenhair won't grow. Zones 4 to 8.

Dwarf Goatsbeard
Aruncus aethusifolius
An enchanting dwarf version of shrub-like goatsbeard, this plant has foamy clusters of creamy-white flowers in late spring. They form dense 6" to 8" clumps of ferny foliage. Grow in moist, neutral to acidic, humus-rich soil in light to full shade. Combine with large leaves for contrast. Zones 4 to 8.

Masterwort
Astrantia major
Deep green, palmately-lobed foliage. Produces open clusters of 1/2" to 1-1/2" starry white or pink flowers on 1' to 2' stems throughout the summer.

The flowers dry well. Plant in moist to wet, neutral, humus-rich soil in light to partial shade. Plants tolerate full sun in cooler zones. Combine with bold plants such as *Ligularia*, hostas and iris. Contrast the foliage with fine textures of sedges, grasses and ferns. Zones 3 to 7.

Variegated Sedge
Carex siderosticta 'Variegata'
The white stripes on the strap-shaped leaves of this 8"-tall sedge brighten up a shaded spot. Plants form broad, dense clumps. Small, fuzzy green flowers in early spring. Plant in moist, neutral to acidic, humus-rich soil in light to full shade. Zones 4 to 8.

Dwarf Goatsbeard

Japanese Roof Iris
Iris tectorum

Indispensable foliage plant with stiff, broad fans of 1-1/2' strap-shaped leaves that persist all season long. Flattened, deep-blue flowers are borne on slender stems in spring. 'Alba' has white flowers. Grow in moist, neutral to acidic, humus-rich soil in sun to partial shade. Plants are extremely drought tolerant but may go dormant under prolonged stress. Use to add lift to low plantings of wildflowers, groundcovers and sedges. Absolutely stunning with the colored foliage of ajuga. Zones 4 to 8.

Loebner Magnolia
Magnolia x *loebneri*

This small- to medium-sized tree, which grows 20' to 30', is noteworthy among magnolias for its cold hardiness. Festooned with white, starry, fragrant flowers in early spring before the leaves emerge. Broadly oval, rich-green leaves turn yellow in autumn. Plant in moist, neutral to acidic soil in full sun or partial shade. Use on the edge of woods, as a specimen tree or as understory in open woods. Zones 4 to 9.

White Comfrey
Symphytum grandiflorum

An overlooked 6"- to 8"-high groundcover with black-green, broadly lance-shaped leaves and nodding creamy-white bells in early spring. Plants form

Loebner Magnolia

broad, weed-proof clumps from creeping stems. Plant in moist, neutral, humus-rich soil in light to deep shade. Plants are drought tolerant. Use under shrubs and small trees or in difficult spots in the roots of canopy trees. Combine with epimediums, hostas, wildflowers and ferns. Zones 3 to 8.

Korean Meadow Rue
Thalictrum ichangense (T. coreanum)

A delightful groundcover with foamy pink flowers throughout the summer on wiry, 4" to 6" stems. Plants have divided leaves with distinctive round or shield-shaped leaflets attached to their stalks in the middle. Plants spread by creeping rhizomes to form dense clumps. They will spread among other plants and pop up here and there. Give them moist, neutral to acidic, humus-rich soil in sun to partial shade. Plant under shrubs or with other shade plants. Zones 4 to 8.

MORE WOODLAND PLANTS FOR THE UPPER MIDWEST

TREES:

Acer saccharum, Sugar Maple
Amelanchier species, Serviceberry, Shadblow
Carya ovata, Shagbark Hickory
Carpinus caroliniana, Musclewood, Ironwood
Magnolia stellata, Star Magnolia
Ostrya virginiana, Hop Hornbeam, Ironwood
Pinus strobus, White Pine
Quercus rubra, Northern Red Oak
Q. macrocarpa, Bur Oak
Tilia americana, Basswood, Linden

SHRUBS AND VINES:

Aronia arbutifolia, Red Chokeberry
Chionanthus virginicus, Fringe Tree
Cornus alternifolia, Red Osier Dogwood
Daphne x *burkwoodii* 'Carol Mackie', Burkwood
   Daphne
Diervilla lonicera, Bush Honeysuckle
Dirca palustris, Leatherwood
Hamamelis virginiana, Witchhazel
Ilex verticillata, Winterberry Holly
Viburnum dentatum, Arrowwood

PERENNIALS:

Actaea species, Baneberry
Aquilegia species and hybrids, Columbine
Anemone ranunculoides, Buttercup Anemone
Anemonella thalictroides, Rue Anemone
Asarum canadense, Wild Ginger
Aster macrophyllus, Bigleaf Aster
Astilbe x *arendsii* and *Astilbe* species, Astilbe
Brunnera macrophylla, Siberian Bugloss
Chelone lyonii and other species, Turtlehead
Cimicifuga racemosa, Black Cohosh
Dicentra eximia, D. spectabilis, Bleeding Heart
Dodecatheon meadia, Shooting Star
Epimedium species and hybrids, Barrenwort
Geranium maculatum, Wild Geranium
G. pratense, Meadow Cranesbill
Helleborus niger, Christmas Rose
Hepatica species, Hepatica
Hosta species and hybrids, Hosta
Iris cristata, Crested Iris
Isopyrum biternatum, Atlantic Isopyrum
Ligularia species, Goldenray, Grounsel
Mertensia virginica, Virginia Bluebells
Phlox stolonifera, Creeping Phlox
Polygonatum odoratum 'Thunbergii',
   Variegated Solomon's-seal
Primula kisoana, Primrose
P. sieboldii, Siebold's Primrose
Pulmonaria species, Lungwort
Stylophorum diphyllum, Celandine Poppy
Tiarella cordifolia, Foamflower
Tricyrtis species, Toadlily
Zizia aptera, Heart-leaf Alexander

GRASSES AND GRASSLIKE PLANTS:

Carex species, Sedges

FERN:

Polystichum setiferum, Soft Shield Fern

THE NORTHEAST
ZONES 3 TO 7

The Northeast is characterized by a wide range of winter temperatures, from around 10°F in Zone 7 to as low as -40°F in Zone 3. Inland and upland areas can expect regular snow cover; parts of zones 5, 6 and 7 cannot. Rainfall is about 42 inches per year, coming principally in the spring and fall, which means that woodland gardens may need supplemental water during summer. Soils are variable even within a site, but are typically rocky, shallow, acidic and somewhat deficient in phosphorus. To support a diverse collection of plants in competition with trees, the soil must be constantly improved.

15 GREAT WOODLAND PLANTS FOR THE NORTHEAST

NATIVE:

White Baneberry, Doll's Eyes
Actaea pachypoda
Wonderful 1'- to 3'-tall hoopskirted member of the buttercup family. Showy white flowers followed by spectacular, long-lasting displays of decorative (but poisonous) white berries on red stems. Mass in cool, moist areas. *Actaea rubra,* Red baneberry, is earlier-ripening, with patent-leather red fruits. Zones 2 to 8.

Plantain-leaved Sedge, Seersucker Sedge
Carex plantaginea
Strongly ribbed and puckered bright-green rosettes, to about 12". Yellow-brown flower spikes in spring. Evergreen; a good native alternative to hostas. Prefers a cool spot in partial to full shade. Multiplies rapidly. Zones 4 to 8.

White Baneberry

Shooting Star
Dodecatheon meadia
Enchanting spring ephemeral, with flowers from magenta to white flaring out like shooting stars behind clustered stamens. Foliage disappears by mid-summer, leaving ripening seed receptacles. Combine with lamium 'White Nancy', which enjoys the same humus-rich soil and partial shade. Zones 4 to 8.

Coral Bells, Alum Root
Heuchera americana
A 1'-tall mounding plant with persistent red foliage strongly veined with silver. Flowers are insignficant. Divide rhizomes every four to five years. Prefers well-drained soil rich in organic matter. Zones 4 to 9

Turk's-cap Lily
Lilium superbum
Sturdy, 6' tall. Topped in late July by numerous orange-scarlet bells. Foliage arranged around the stem in handsome whorls. Spreads rapidly. Seedheads make dramatic accents. Prefers filtered light and a moist, well-drained, somewhat acidic soil. *Lilium canadense,* Canada lily is slightly earlier, more delicate looking but hardier. Zones 4 to 8.

Christmas Fern
Polystichum acrostichoides
A clumping evergreen fern, dark and lustrous. A good accent when used in groups. Emerging fiddleheads are dramatic, silvery haired. Adapts to many sites—rocky, sandy, swampy, shade or semi-shade. Zones 3 to 8.

Double Bloodroot
Sanguinaria canadensis 'Multiplex'
A stunning treasure, with many pure white petals cupped as though holding a chalice in early spring. Heavily veined leaves. Distinctively lobed blue-

Double Bloodroot

green foliage is handsome all summer, wonderful massed. This cultivar is sterile, so its rhizome must be divided in August if you want to enjoy it in quantities. Requires a moisture-retentive, well-drained soil. Zones 3 to 8.

Redvein Enkianthus

NON-NATIVE:

Astilbe
Astilbe simplicifolia 'Hennie Graafland'
Soft pink flowers July to August.
Glossy, finely cut, bronzed foliage.
Best in moist soils. The native *A. biternata* soars to 4' and has pure white
flowers in July. Zones 3 to 8.

Umbrella Leaf
Diphylleia cymosa
Grows to 2-1/2' tall from stout, easily
divided rhizomes. Large-lobed leaf,
like an opened bivalve, may grow to 2'
across. Small white flowers are followed by sprays of persistent blue fruit
on showy red stems. Moist soils.
Zones 4 to 7.

Redvein Enkianthus
Enkianthus campanulatus
Small tree, to about 15'. Elegant narrow, upright form, layered branches
and smoky-gray, fine-textured bark
offer winter interest. Dainty redveined, bell-shaped flowers in May to
June. Attractive, shiny seed clusters.
Magnificent fall color. Zones 5 to 7.

Barrenwort
Epimedium species, hybrids and cultivars
An indispensable group of plants,
often mislabeled. Habit may be
spreading or clumping; texture coarse
or dainty. Plants range from 8" to 15"
tall. Flowers may be pink, lavender,

Bethlehem Sage, Spotted Lungwort

Rodger's Flower

Bethlehem Sage, Spotted Lungwort
Pulmonaria saccharata
Long-lived, dependable plants, 8" to 10" tall. Long-lasting pink or blue bells in early spring. Exciting foliage marked with white spots is very persistent. Prefers cool, moist soil. Pretty woodland groundcover. *P. s.* 'Mrs. Moon' forms mounded rosette, *P. s.* 'Roy Davidson' has narrow leaves, upright form. Many other forms available. Zones 4 to 7.

Rodger's Flower
Rodgersia aesculifolia
Bold, arresting plant to 4' tall. Forms large clumps. Big, palmately compound leaves, wonderful bronze color in early

low or orange, variable in size. Foliage may be deciduous or persistent. Favorites include *E. grandiflorum* 'Lilafee', *E.* x *warleyense*, *E.* x *youngianum* 'Niveum' and *E.* x *rubrum*. Easy to grow. Zones 4 to 8.

Hake
Hakonechloa macra 'Aureola'
Brilliant yellow deciduous grass with green stripes, very slow to establish. The 12" leaves arch over gracefully; flowers are open panicles, effective in late summer. Needs humus-rich soil. Zones 5 to 9.

Shuttlecock Flower
Kirengeshoma palmata
3' to 4' shrubby perennial. Paired maple-like leaves. Round buds are effective long before the soft yellow flowers open in September. Needs rich, moist soil. Zones 4 to 8.

Umbrella Leaf

spring. Creamy white flowers in long panicles in June, followed by decorative seed heads. Quick to increase in moist, rich soils. Zones 5 to 7.

87

MORE WOODLAND PLANTS FOR THE NORTHEAST

TREES:

Amelanchier x *grandiflora*, Serviceberry, Shad
Cercis canadensis 'Alba', White Redbud
Cornus kousa, Kousa Dogwood
Halesia tetraptera, Silverbell
Ilex opaca, American Holly
Magnolia virginiana, Sweet Bay
Stewartia pseudocamellia, Japanese Stewartia
Styrax japonicus, Japanese Silverbell

SHRUBS AND VINES:

Clethra alnifolia 'Rosea', Sweet Pepperbush
Fothergilla gardenii, Bottlebrush Shrub
Hydrangea anomala ssp. *petiolaris*, Climbing
   Hydrangea
H. quercifolia, Oakleaf Hydrangea
Leucothoë fontanesiana, Hobblebush
Mahonia 'King's Ransom', Oregon Grape Holly
Rhododendron bakeri, Cumberland Azalea
R. vaseyi, Vaseyi or Pinkshell Azalea
Viburnum alnifolium, Hobblebush Viburnum
Xanthorhiza simplicissima, Yellowroot

PERENNIALS:

Anemonopsis macrophylla, False Anemone
Arisaema triphyllum, Jack-in-the-Pulpit
Aruncus dioicus, Goat's Beard
Asarum europaeum, European Ginger
Chelone obliqua, Rose Turtlehead
Chrysogonum virginianum, Green and Gold

Cimicifuga racemosa, Fairy Candles, Bugbane,
   Rattlebox
Dodecatheon species, Shooting Star
Darmera peltata, Umbrella Leaf
Erythronium 'Pagoda', Pagoda Trout Lily
Gentiana clausa, Bottle Gentian
Geranium macrorrhizum, Cranesbill
Gillenia trifoliata (Porteranthus trifoliata),
   Bowman's Root
Helleborus niger, Christmas Rose
Iris cristata 'Alba', Crested Wood Iris
Lobelia siphilitica, Great Blue Lobelia
Ligularia stenocephala 'The Rocket'
Mertensia virginica, Virginia Bluebells
Patrinia scabiosifolia
Peltoboykinia watanabei, Peltoboykinia
Penstemon smallii, Small's Penstemon
Polygonatum commutatum, Giant Solomon's-seal
P. odoratum 'Thunbergii', Variegated
   Solomon's-seal
Primula polyanthus, Primrose
Scutellaria serrata, Showy Skullcap
Thalictrum rochebrunianum, Meadow Rue
Tricyrtis hirta, Hairy Toad-Lily
Vancouveria hexandra, Inside-out Flower
Zizia aptera, Golden Alexanders

GRASSES AND GRASSLIKE PLANTS:

Carex pendula, Drooping Sedge
Chasmanthium latifolium, Northern Wild Oats

FERNS:

Adiantum pedatum, Maidenhair Fern
Dryopteris filix-mas, Male Fern
D. goldiana, Goldie's Fern
Matteuccia pensylvanica, Ostrich Fern

THE ROCKY MOUNTAINS
ZONES 4 TO 5

The Rocky Mountain region is marked by a diversity of climates and weather extremes, including severe winter winds, intense winter sun, periods of drought, summer hail storms and low humidity. In autumn, the temperature can drop suddenly 75 degrees in less than 12 hours. The growing season in the Rocky Mountains is shorter than in other parts of the country, there are more hours of sunlight and its intensity is greater because of the altitude. A plant that may need full sun in other parts of the country can be grown here in partial shade.

15 GREAT WOODLAND PLANTS FOR THE ROCKY MOUNTAINS

NATIVE:

Pussytoes
Antennaria parvifolia
Evergreen groundcover. Delicate, small rosettes form a silvery mat, 2" to 3" tall. Tiny white flower heads on 2"- to 6"-tall stems. Drought tolerant. Pretty when planted between stepping stones. Grow in light shade. Zones 4 to 8.

Rocky Mountain Columbine
Aquilegia caerulea
Blue or lavender and white flowers 2" to 4" across in spring with spurs 1" to 2" long. Stout flower stems 1' to 2' tall. Deeply divided leaves. Grow in moist, well drained soil. Susceptible to aphids. Zones 3 to 7 .

Kinnikinick
Arctostaphylos uva-ursi
Woody, trailing, evergreen groundcover, 3" to 6" tall, forming a rich, dark-green carpet 3' across. Leathery, shiny, bright-green leaves. Waxy, dainty, vase-shaped pinkish-white flowers in late winter; bright crimson berries in the fall. Grow in well-drained neutral or acidic soil; slow to establish but well worth the wait. Zones 3 to 8.

Rocky Mountain Columbine

Colorado Male Fern

Colorado Male Fern
Dryopteris filix-mas
Unlike the Eastern species, this fern only reaches 2' tall. Erect, dark-green, lance shaped, leathery fronds grow to 6" wide. Semi-evergreen with a spreading habit. Sun tolerant if planted in moist soil rich in organic matter. *D. f.-m.* 'Barnesii' is a pretty cultivar with ruffled fronds. Zone 3 to 7.

Coral Bells
Heuchera sanguinea
Evergreen, compact mound with round, scalloped, leathery basal leaves. Forms clumps up to 10" wide. Bright red bells on wiry stems up to 20" long most of the summer. Good for the woodland edge. Popular cultivars are available with white, pink or deep scarlet flowers. Species for the shady rock garden, all with greenish flowers, are *H. richardsonii,* (Alumroot), *H. bracteata* and *H. hallii*. Zones 4 to 8.

Waxflower
Jamesia americana
Deciduous shrub to 4' tall. Small, gray, felted leaves with scalloped edges. Good shape and form. Attractive bark. Waxy, fragrant white flowers in spring. In the fall, leaves turn shades of rose and dark red. Plant in partial shade in rich, well-drained, soil or decomposed granite. Zones 4 to 7.

Creeping Holly Berry
Mahonia repens
Broad-leaved evergreen groundcover growing to 1' to 1-1/2' tall. Compact and dense. Glossy, hollylike leaves and plump clusters of yellow flowers in spring. Black-purple fruit. Fall leaf color is light to deep red. Drought tolerant. Good groundcover for difficult areas. Low maintenance; prefers well-drained soil and needs protection from winter sun and wind. Zones 3 to 8.

Coral Bells

Pasque Flower

Plume Flower
Astilbe chinensis var. *pumila*
Deciduous, upright bushy mound, to 1' tall. Lacy, fern-like, deeply divided leaves are dark green. Stiff, 8" to 10" high bottlebrush-like spikes of luminous pink to lavender blossoms in late summer or early fall. Plant at the woodland edge in moisture-retentive soil that is well drained in winter. Makes a good groundcover. Zones 4 to 8.

Pasque Flower
Pulsatilla patens
One of the earliest spring flowers, 4" wide, lavender to blue and deep purple underneath with gold centers. Grows to 8" tall. Finely divided, hairy leaves appear after flowering. Fluffy, mop-like seed heads are attractive for months. Requires shade through the heat of the day and good drainage. Zones 4 to 7.

NON-NATIVE:

European Wild Ginger
Asarum europaeum
Evergreen groundcover growing to 6" tall and spreading to 12". Glossy, leathery dark green leaves are either heart shaped or kidney shaped, 3" wide. This plant is grown for its pretty leaves. *A. hartwegii,* another attractive ginger, has larger leaves with silver veins. Zones 4 to 8.

Perennial Forget-me-not
Brunnera macrophylla
Dark green, heart-shaped leaves 6" to 8" wide. Forms attractive mounds. Airy sprays of bright blue flowers in early spring. Grows to 18" tall. Self sows freely; share young seedlings with gardening friends. Grow in ordinary soil in full sun to partial shade. A favorite spring flower. Zones 3 to 8.

Baby Cyclamen
Cyclamen hederifolium
Slow-spreading groundcover. Thick, glossy, pale-green leaves with attractive silver mottling are lightly serrated, heart-shaped and grow to 3" across. Leaves disappear in early summer but return in late fall. Small, downward-facing flowers appear on 4"-tall, single wiry stems in fall. Flowers are pale to deep pink, stained darker around the mouth, or white. Plant in well-drained soil rich in organic matter. Zones 5 to 8.

Foxglove

3' to 4'. Leaves can be long and narrow, heart shaped or round, with green, blue, gold or variegated foliage. Flower spikes are usually blue, lavender or white; many are fragrant. Needs rich, moist, well drained soil. Zones 3 to 8.

Foxglove
Digitalis species
Perennials or biennials, 4' to 5' tall. Basal rosettes of long, narrow leaves with upright flower stalks covered with bell shaped flowers. *D. grandiflora* has 2"-long yellow flowers; *D.* x *mertonensis* has large pink flowers; *D. lutea* is 3' tall with tiny yellow flowers; *D. purpurea* has lavender, purple-pink, rose or white flowers. Prefers fertile, well-drained soil in partial shade. Zones 4 to 8.

Plantain-lily
Hosta species or cultivars
Long-lived perennial; one of the most popular foliage plants for shade. Various sizes, from the very small *H. venusta,* 4" tall with narrow 1" leaves, to *H. sieboldiana,* which can spread to

Musk Mallow
Malva moschata
Glossy, deep emerald green, deeply divided foliage that forms a bushy rosette. Rose-mauve hollyhock-like flowers are 2" wide on 2' stalks, from midsummer for six to eight weeks. Needs light shade or early morning sun. Easy to grow by scattering seed in the fall. *M.m.* 'Alba', with pure white flowers, is prettier grown in light shade. Zones 3 to 8.

Hostas

MORE WOODLAND PLANTS FOR THE ROCKY MOUNTAINS

TREES:

Amelanchier species, Serviceberry
Celtis occidentalis, Hackberry
Cercis canadensis, Redbud
Cornus mas, Cornelian Cherry, Dogwood
Corylus colurna, Turkish Filbert
Phellodendron amurense, Amur Cork Tree
Ptelea trifoliata, Wafer Ash
Quercus macrocarpa, Bur Oak
Q. robur, English Oak
Tilia americana, American Linden
T. cordata, Littleleaf Linden

SHRUBS AND VINES:

Cotoneaster horizontalis, Rockspray
Daphne species, Daphne
Hypericum patulum 'Hidcote', St. John's Wort
Hydrangea arborescens 'Annabelle', Annabelle Hydrangea
Kerria japonica 'Picta', Japanese Kerria
Ribes aureum, Golden Currant
Rosa glauca (rubrifolia), Red Leaf Shrub Rose
Rubus deliciosus, Boulder Raspberry
Sorbaria sorbifolia, False Spirea
Symphoricarpos occidentalis, Snow Berry
Viburnum trilobum, Cranberry Bush

PERENNIALS:

Acanthus mollis, Bear's Breech
Actaea rubra, Western Red Baneberry
Alchemilla mollis, Lady's-mantle
Arum italicum, Italian Arum
Anemone canadensis, Canada Anemone
A. sylvestris, Snowdrop Anemone
Bergenia cordifolia, Heartleaf Bergenia
Campanula persicifolia, Peach-leaf Bellflower
Cynoglossum nervosum, Hairy Hound's Tongue
Epimedium versicolor 'Sulphureum', Barrenwort
Galium odoratum, Sweet Woodruff
Geranium macrorrhizum, Bigroot Geranium
Helleborus orientalis, Lenten Rose
Iris cristata, Crested Iris
Lamium maculatum, Creeping Nettle
Mertensia lanceolata, Bluebell
Omphalodes verna, Blue-eyed Mary
Penstemon digitalis 'Husker Red', Foxglove Penstemon
Phlox stolonifera, Creeping Phlox
Primula elatior, Primrose
Pulmonaria saccharata, Lungwort
Tellima grandiflora, Fringecups
Tiarella cordifolia, Foamflower
Verbascum phoeniceum, Purple Mullein
Veronica filiformis, Birdseye Veronica
Vinca minor, Periwinkle

FERNS:

Adiantum aleuticum 'Subpumilum', Western Maidenhair, dwarf form
Athyrium nipponicum 'Pictum', Japanese Painted Fern
Dryopteris goldiana, Goldie's Fern
Gymnocarpium dryopteris, Oak Fern
G. robertianum, Limestone Oak Fern
Polystichum setiferum, Soft Shield Fern

THE PACIFIC NORTHWEST
ZONES 4 TO 7

The climate of the Pacific Northwest is characterized by relatively cool and dry summers and mild, wet winters. The lack of soil moisture under the predominant masts of needled evergreens is by far the most limiting factor for gardening in these sites. Although it's not uncommon to have short bouts of extremely cold temperatures that drift southward from the Arctic in winter, a high overstory of trees will often help protect both woody and herbaceous plants. The mineral soils are diverse in texture throughout the region, although they share a common deficiency in nitrogen and are slightly acidic by nature. Sandy soils must be amended with organic matter to increase water-holding capacity, whereas clay soils can be amended with coarse sand or organic matter to increase tilth.

15 GREAT WOODLAND PLANTS FOR THE PACIFIC NORTHWEST

NATIVE:

Western Wild Ginger
Asarum caudatum
A delightful, underused groundcover with dark, 3" oval leaves held slightly above the soil surface, rising from a spreading mat of ginger-scented rhizomes. Intriguing brownish-red flowers in early spring beneath the foliage. Grow in light shade in moderately dry soil. Zones 4 to 8.

Low Oregon Grape
Mahonia nervosa
Broadleaved evergreen shrub with 2' to 3' stems cloaked with large compound leaves, each composed of anywhere from nine to 11 jagged-edged leaflets of dark, glossy green in shade, or burgundy under brighter conditions. Erect, 8" panicles of clear yellow flowers in early spring, followed by succulent dark blue berries blushed with white. Grow in light shade in well-drained soils; drought tolerant. Zones 5 to 7.

Mountain Box Shrub

Western Trillium

neat, tidy mounds. Will reseed itself throughout the woodland. Erect white or pink-blushed flowers in April and May. Foliage attractive throughout the year. Prefers well-drained soils in light shade. Zones 3 to 8.

Western Trillium
Trillium ovatum
Graces the early spring woodland with white, slightly nodding flowers on 8" stems. Grows slowly to form fine clumps, each with dozens of flowers. Goes dormant in early summer. There is an extremely rare double-flowered form. Drought tolerant. Plant in spring in moist, but well-drained soil in light shade. Zones 4 to 8.

Evergreen Huckleberry
Vaccinium ovatum
Handsome native shrub that grows to 6' tall over time. Small, oval-shaped dark green leaves along stems that are red when young. In late spring, clusters of pinkish white, bell-shaped flowers are produced in abundance, followed in late summer by tart, shiny black berries. Grow in moderately shaded areas with acidic, well-drained soil. Drought tolerant once established. Zones 6 to 9.

Evergreen Vancouveria
Vancouveria planipetala
A durable, spreading groundcover with glossy evergreen foliage. Grows in dry shade. Spreads slowly to form large,

Mountain Box Shrub
Paxistima myrtifolia (*P. myrsinites*)
Evergreen shrub that grows up to 3' tall. Small, highly textural glossy green leaves and small clusters of reddish brown flowers in midspring. Prefers well-drained, acidic soils; tolerates drought and very deep shade. Zones 5 to 8.

Sword Fern
Polystichum munitum
One of the best ferns for western woodlands. Will eventually create sizable clumps of evergreen fronds to 4' tall and wide. Easily transplanted at any time of the year. Cut back three times a year to keep a tidier appearance. Prefers well-drained soils, but will tolerate some moisture. Very adaptable. Zones 5 to 9.

Foamflower
Tiarella trifoliata
Exceptional woodland plant. Forms

weed-suppressing colonies to 8" tall. Airy sprays of white flowers are held above the foliage in early to mid spring. Another native, *V. hexandra,* is deciduous, with more finely textured foliage. Grow in well-drained soil in light shade. Zones 4 to 8.

NON-NATIVE:

Striped Maple, Goosefoot Maple
Acer pensylvanicum
Tree, to 20' tall. One of many maples known as the stripe-bark or snake-bark maples, because the bark is striated with fine lines of white and gray-green. Bark remains attractive even on older trees in shade, but becomes scorched and unsightly in full sun. Bold, bright-green spring and summer

Striped Maple, Goosefoot Maple

leaves take on soft yellow tints in autumn. Tolerant of moist and dry soils alike, easily grown in light shade. Zones 4 to 8.

White Wood Aster
Aster divaricatus
Native to the eastern coast of North America, the wood aster performs admirably in the Pacific Northwest as well. Black, wiry stems hold dark green foliage and grow to 18". In mid summer profuse small white flowers appear, brightening the woodland floor in a long display of bloom. Will self sow in difficult sites. Prefers light shade. Zones 4 to 8.

Disanthus
Disanthus cercidifolius
A large, multistemmed shrub that grows to 10' tall over time. One of the finest shrubs available for autumn color, with striking hues of clarets and oranges even in full shade. Heart-shaped foliage. Small red flowers, resembling those of the witchhazels, in late autumn. Prefers well-drained but moist, rich soils in light shade. Zones 6 to 8.

Miss Robb's Spurge
Euphorbia amygdaloides var. *robbiae*
One of the few evergreen groundcovers that establishes well in dry shade, including under the western red cedar. Large, quickly forming colonies of 8" stems are cloaked with splendid

Disanthus cercidifolius

green foliage provide a handsome vertical accent. Extremely tolerant of dry shade. Zones 6 to 9.

Wheel Tree
Trochodendron aralioides
Broadleaved evergreen tree that grows slowly to 25'. Whorls of glossy green foliage crown the ends of branches that are aligned in a tiered fashion along the trunk. Foliage takes on hints of russet in winter. In early spring, intriguing green flowers that look like small parasols form in clusters at the ends of branches. Grow in light shade, in rich, well-drained soil. Zones 7 to 9.

dark green leaves. In early spring, chartreuse flowers unfurl from the tip of each stem and rise to 18". Extremely drought tolerant. Zones 5 to 8.

Garden Hydrangea
Hydrangea macrophylla
Brings color to the woodland garden late in the season. Many cultivars are available, both with large mophead flower clusters and more delicate lacecaps, in colors ranging from pure white to pinks, reds and blue. Hydrangeas will blossom more profusely when grown in light shade with moderate amounts of water during the growing season. Zones 6 to 10.

Gladwyn Iris
Iris foetidissima
Grown not so much for its light lavender flowers, as for its tangerine-colored fruit, which tumbles from swollen green pods in late summer through early winter. Glossy swords of ever-

Garden Hydrangea

MORE WOODLAND PLANTS FOR THE PACIFIC NORTHWEST

TREES:

Acer crataegifolium 'Veitchii', Variegated Hawthorn Maple

A. davidii, David's Maple

A. tegmentosum, Manchu-striped Maple

Robinia pseudoacacia 'Frisia', Black Locust

SHRUBS AND VINES:

Aucuba japonica, Japanese Aucuba

Camellia oleifera, Camellia

C. sasanqua, Camellia

C. sinensis, Tea Camellia

C. x *williamsii*, Camellia

Clethra barbinervis, Japanese Clethra

Daphne laureola, Spurge Daphne

Gaultheria shallon, Salal

Hydrangea anomala var. *petiolaris*, Climbing Hydrangea

H. aspera, H. a. 'Robusta'

H. sargentiana, Sargent Hydrangea

Mahonia 'Arthur Menzies', Mahonia

Rubus parviflorus 'Double Form', Double-formed Thimble Berry

R. spectabilis 'Olympic Double', Double-formed Salmon Berry

Schizophragma hydrangeoides

Vaccinium parvifolium Red Huckleberry

PERENNIALS:

Aquilegia vulgaris 'Variegata', Variegated Columbine

Aralia racemosa, American Spikenard

A. cordata, Japanese Spikenard

A. californica, Elk Clover

Aruncus dioicus, Goatsbeard

Astrantia major, Masterwort

Cimicifuga racemosa, C. japonica, C. simplex, Bugbanes

Corydalis flexuosa, Blue Corydalis

Cyclamen hederifolium

Disporum hookeri, D. smithii, D. sessile, Fairybells

Epimedium species and cultivars, Bishop's Cap

Erythronium species, Trout Lilies, Glacier Lilies

Fuchsia magellanica and hardy hybrids, Fuchsia

Galanthus species, Snowdrops

Galax urceolata, Wand Flower

Gentiana species, Gentian

Geranium macrorrhizum

G. maculatum, Spotted Geranium, Wild Geranium

Geranium phaeum, Mourning Widow Geranium

Gillenia trifoliata, Bowman's Root

Helleborus argutifolius, Corsican Hellebore

H. niger, Christmas Rose

H. x *hybridus*, Lenten Rose

H. x *sternii*

Hosta species, Hostas

Lamium maculatum, Dead Nettle

Meconopsis betonicifolia, M. grandis, M. napaulensis, Asiatic Poppies

Mitella breweri, Miterwort

Omphalodes verna, O. cappadocica, Navelwort

Pachyphragma macrophylla

Pachysandra procumbens, P. terminalis, P. stylosa, Spurge

Polygonatum humile, Solomon's-seal

Primula species, Primrose

Pulmonaria longifolia, Lungwort

P. montana, Lungwort

P. saccharata, Jerusalem Sage

Shortia galacifolia, Shortia or Oconee Bells

Smilacina racemosa, False Solomon's-seal

Soldanella species, Soldanella

Symphytum grandiflorum, Comfrey

S. x 'Goldsmith', Variegated Comfrey

S. x 'Hidcote Blue', Hidcote Blue Comfrey

Trachystemon orientalis

GRASSES:

Luzula sylvatica, Woodrush

THE DEEP SOUTH
ZONES 8 TO 9

The deep South—the area from Eastern Texas across Louisiana through southern Mississippi, Alabama and Georgia as well as eastern South and North Carolina—has an average minimum winter temperature of 10 to 20°F, although normal lows fall in the 30s. Winter temperatures can plummet 30 degrees in an afternoon, which can be destructive to many tender plant species. Daily summer temperatures average in the mid 90s. Rainfall is heavy, with a yearly average of 50 to 60 inches. Soils are generally heavy and acidic on a dense clay base.

15 GREAT WOODLAND PLANTS FOR THE DEEP SOUTH

NATIVE:

Chalkbark Maple
Acer leucoderme, (A. saccharum leucoderme)
Small tree to 25' tall. Southern variation of sugar maple. Fine twigging, smooth bark and elegant structure make it a good substitute for Japanese maple. Grow in loose woodland soil in high shade. Drought tolerant. Vibrant salmon-yellow fall color. Zones 5 to 9.

Paw Paw
Asimina triloba
Dramatic, coarse-textured deciduous tree to 20' tall and wide. Curious purplish-brown flowers attached directly to the branches before or with the new leaves in spring. Interesting banana-flavored fruit in fall. Excellent yellow fall foliage color. Prefers loose, fertile woodland soil, shade and average moisture. Readily accepts smaller plants at its base. Zones 5 to 8.

Summersweet Clethra
Clethra alnifolia
Deciduous shrub to 7' tall. Suckers

Chalkbark Maple

and forms manageable colonies. Deep-green, substantial foliage. Yellow and golden-brown fall foliage. Sweetly scented white flowers in summer. Prefers moist, well-drained soil in sun to partial shade; tolerates wet soils. Zones 3 to 9.

Oakleaf Hydrangea
Hydrangea quercifolia
Striking, rounded deciduous shrub 6' by 6'. Coarse-textured, oak-like foliage turns red or orange-brown to purple in fall. Conspicuous large panicles of white flowers up to 12" long in late spring. Exfoliating cinnamon-brown bark is showy in winter. Various cultivars have showier flowers than the species. A dwarf form is also available. Requires exceptionally good drainage and partial shade. Zones 5 to 9.

Oakleaf Hydrangea

Starbush or Florida Anise
Illicium floridanum
Tidy, upright, evergreen shrub to 10'. Leathery leaves exude a curious fragrance when crushed. Unique maroon-purple flowers in spring followed by multi-pointed star-like fruit in fall. A subtle plant whose character becomes more insistent as you live with it. Requires excellent drainage, in shade or partial sun. Zones 7 to 9.

Needle Palm
Rhapidophyllum hystrix
Striking clump palm native to the southern coastal plain, to 5' or 6' tall and wide. Shiny fan-shaped leaves to 2-1/2' radiate out from the short trunk, which is covered with sharp, erect needles deserving respect. Prefers low, wet areas in deep shade; also tolerates sun. Hardy to -6°F. Zones 7 to 10.

Piedmont Azalea
Rhododendron canescens
Deciduous shrub usually no more than 10' tall. Rangy and open, its unique sympodial branching is a highlight in winter. Most noted for symmetrical clusters of white to pink, fragrant, honeysuckle-like flowers in midspring. Many fine hybrids have been developed, expanding the color palette. Requires good drainage, with light shade for full flowering. Zones 5 to 9.

Piedmont Azalea

Arrowwood Viburnum
Viburnum dentatum
Strong, tree-like or multi-stemmed deciduous shrub growing to 15' tall. Lustrous, toothed leaves turn yellow to salmon to reddish purple in fall. Ornamental branch structure provides interest in winter, and abundant, showy clusters of creamy white flowers appear in late spring. Grow in moist, sandy loam in full sun to partial shade. Zones 2 to 8.

Netted Chain Fern
Woodwardia (Lorinseria) areolata
Small fern with erect, relatively coarse dark green leaves and erect fruiting structure that turns black and lasts into winter. Durable, slow spreading; a good groundcover in moist areas in sun or shade. Zones 3 to 9.

NON-NATIVE:

Christmas Berry
Ardisia crenata
Lustrous, small evergreen shrub; erect habit to 3'. Scalloped-edged dark green foliage. Clusters of white flowers in spring and early summer, followed by berries that turn red in December and persist throughout winter. Slow growing but long lived. Appreciates protection of evergreen trees. When older plants fall over, cut stems back to the ground and replacements will develop. Zones 8 to 10.

Japanese Camellia
Camellia japonica
Favorite evergreen flowering shrub of the South. Slow growing, typically to 6' to 8' tall though much larger with age. Consistently upright in habit. Rich

Christmas Berry

selection of flower forms and colors blooming from early winter to late spring. Small-flowered varieties and those with single flowers and conspicuous stamens seem more natural. Good drainage required. Zones 7 to 9.

Pineapple Lily
Curcuma species
A tropical genus of ginger well adapted to the lower South. Coarse-textured, herbaceous plant growing from a cold-resistant rhizome producing large, erect, banana-like leaves. 2' to 10' tall, depending on the species. Unique, late spring and summer inflorescences of erect, showy pink to maroon bracts with small yellow flowers. Recommended species from the lowest to the tallest include *C. petiolata, C. zedoaria, C. elata* and *C. latifolia.* Grow in moist soil rich in organic matter, in sun or partial shade. Zones 8 to 10.

Butterfly Ginger

Butterfly Ginger
Hedychium species and hybrids
Striking, fast-growing tropical perennials, 6' to 7' tall. Vigorous, easily divided rhizomes produce several erect, coarse-leaved stems terminating in a showy cluster of very fragrant flowers during summer and fall. Colors include white, yellow, pink, orange-red, salmon and rose. Excellent for cutting. Prefers moist, rich soil in full sun to partial shade. Zones 8 to 10.

Chinese Evergreen Witchhazel
Loropetalum chinense
Upright and arching evergreen shrub with small, leathery, dark green leaves. Open structure emphasizes the plant's sculptural form. Many small white, strap-like flowers in early spring. A new cultivar with rich pink flowers and purplish-green foliage is striking. Moderate growth; requires four to five years before signficant bloom begins. Moist, well-drained soil in full sun to partial shade. Zones 8 to 9.

Blue Japanese Oak
Quercus glauca
Glossy, dense evergreen oak to 40' tall. Striking leaves are olive green above and gray-blue below. Beautiful form with smooth gray bark and low horizontal branching. Prefers a fertile, well-drained soil in sun or high shade; will tolerate heat and dryness. Leaves do not wilt in temperatures as low as 10°F. Zones 8 to 9.

MORE WOODLAND PLANTS FOR THE DEEP SOUTH

TREES:

Acer palmatum, Japanese Maple
Crataegus marshallii, Parsley Hawthorn
Cyrilla racemiflora, Titi
Halesia diptera, Silver-bell
Ilex vomitoria, Yaupon
Magnolia grandiflora, Southern Magnolia
M. stellata, Star Magnolia
M. tripetala, Umbrella Magnolia
Michelia figo, Banana Shrub
M. x *foggii*, Michelia
Prunus caroliniana, Cherry Laurel
Rhamnus caroliniana, Carolina Buckthorn
Ulmus crassifolia, Cedar Elm

SHRUBS AND VINES:

Agarista populifolia, Florida Leucothoe
Callicarpa americana, French Mulberry
C. dichotoma, Purple Beautyberry
Calycanthus floridus, Carolina Allspice
Camellia sasanqua, Sasanqua Camellia
Cephalotaxus harringtonia, Japanese Plum Yew
Euonymus americanus, Strawberry Bush
Hamamelis virginiana, Eastern Witchhazel
Hydrangea arborescens, Mountain Hydrangea
Gardenia thunbergia, Hip Gardenia
Illicium parviflorum, Small Anise-tree
Indigofera kirilowii, Indigo
Itea virginica, Virginia Willow
Ligustrum sinense 'Variegatum', Variegated
   Chinese Privet
Mahonia bealei, Leatherleaf Mahonia
Osmanthus fragrans 'Aurantiacus',
   Orange-flowered Sweet Olive

Pittosporum tobira 'Variegata', Variegated
   Pittosporum
Rhododendron austrinum, Flame Azalea
R. indicum cultivars, Indian Azalea
Ternstroemia gymnanthera and 'Variegata',
   Green and Variegated Cleyeras
Viburnum japonicum, Japanese Viburnum
V. nudum, Swamp Viburnum

PERENNIALS:

Alpinia japonica, Dwarf Ginger
Ardisia japonica, Japanese Ardisia
Aspidistra elatior and 'Variegata', Green and
   Variegated Cast Iron Plants
Colocasia esculenta cultivars, Elephant's Ear
Crinum species and hybrids, Crinum Lily
Hosta species and cultivars, Hosta
Ligularia tussilaginea and cultivars, Evergreen
   Ligularia
Liriope muscari 'Evergreen Giant' and 'Aztec',
   Giant and Variegated Liriopes
Petasites japonicus, Japanese Butterbur
Podophyllum peltatum, May Apple
Rohdea japonica and cultivars, Green and
   Variegated Rohdeas

GRASSES AND GRASSLIKE PLANTS:

Carex pendula, Drooping Sedge

FERNS:

Athyrium asplenioides (A. filix-femina var.
   asplenioides), Southern Lady Fern
Cyrtomium falcatum, Holly Fern
Diplazium esculentum, Oriental Vegetable Fern
Osmunda regalis, Royal Fern

HARDINESS ZONES

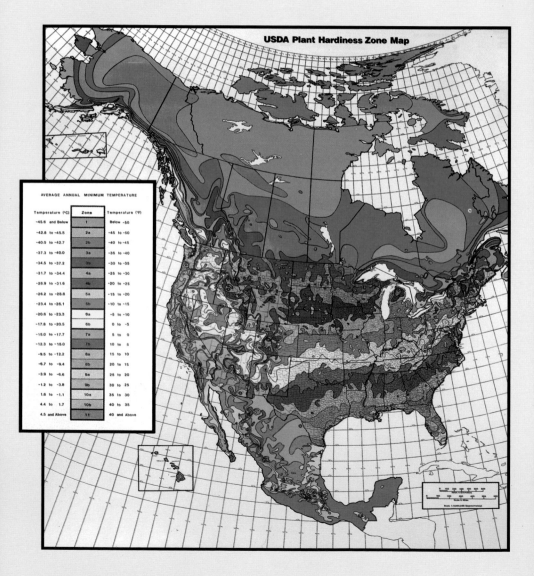

USDA Plant Hardiness Zone Map

Temperature (°C)	Zone	Temperature (°F)
-45.6 and Below	1	Below -50
-42.8 to -45.5	2a	-45 to -50
-40.0 to -42.7	2b	-40 to -45
-37.3 to -40.0	3a	-35 to -40
-34.5 to -37.2	3b	-30 to -35
-31.7 to -34.4	4a	-25 to -30
-28.9 to -31.6	4b	-20 to -25
-26.2 to -28.8	5a	-15 to -20
-23.4 to -26.1	5b	-10 to -15
-20.6 to -23.3	6a	-5 to -10
-17.8 to -20.5	6b	0 to -5
-15.0 to -17.7	7a	5 to 0
-12.3 to -15.0	7b	10 to 5
-9.5 to -12.2	8a	15 to 10
-6.7 to -9.4	8b	20 to 15
-3.9 to -6.6	9a	25 to 20
-1.2 to -3.8	9b	30 to 25
1.6 to -1.1	10a	35 to 30
4.4 to 1.7	10b	40 to 35
4.5 and Above	11	40 and Above

AVERAGE ANNUAL MINIMUM TEMPERATURE

CONTRIBUTORS

C. COLSTON BURRELL is a garden designer, writer and photographer. He is president of Native Landscape Design and Restoration, Ltd. of Minneapolis, a design firm specializing in the creation of environmentally appropriate gardens.

ED CLEBSCH is an ecologist and former professor of botany and ecology at the University of Tennessee, Knoxville. He and his wife, Meredith, own and operate Native Gardens, a retail and wholesale nursery in Greenback, Tennessee specializing in herbaceous perennials native to the southeastern states.

GLENN DOUGLAS DREYER is director of the Connecticut College Arboretum in New London, a 440-acre preserve combining natural areas, managed lands and a 20-acre native tree and shrub collection. He is an adjunct associate professor of botany at Connecticut College, and author of *Native Shrubs for Landscaping* and *Connecticut's Notable Trees.*

SUSAN E. DUMAINE is a teacher and lecturer for the New England Wild Flower Society, the Arnold Arboretum and the Massachusetts Horticultural Society. She propagates a range of plants and runs Horticultural Thoughts, a garden consultation and design service.

DANIEL J. HINKLEY owns and operates Heronswood Nursery, near Kingston, Washington and travels extensively abroad collecting plants for trial in his 3-acre garden. A frequent contributor to horticultural publications, he is author of *Winter Ornamentals,* published in 1993 by Sasquatch Press, and is currently writing a book on rare perennials to be published in 1997 by Timber Press.

F M MOOBERRY writes a column on native plants for *The Kennett Paper* and is a designer of native plant landscapes, including gardens at the Brandywine River Museum, Chadds Ford, Pennsylvania. She founded the annual Native Plants in the Landscape conference held at Millersville University, Millersville, Pennsylvania.

BRENDA SKARPHOL is a horticulturist at Green Spring Gardens Park in Alexandria, Virginia. She's also a horticultural photographer and avid home gardener.

MARY ELLEN TONSING gardens in Littleton, Colorado. She is active in the Rocky Mountain Chapter of the North American Rock Garden Society and a

member of the American Fern Society. She is coordinator of the Satellite
Garden Program for the Hardy Fern Foundation and for the past ten years
has been a volunteer in the Rock Alpine Garden at Denver Botanic Gardens.

WAYNE WOMACK is a professor of landscape architecture at Louisiana State
University in Baton Rouge. A graduate in landscape architecture from LSU
with a Masters in landscape architecture from Harvard University, he is
especially interested in planting design.

ILLUSTRATION CREDITS

Drawings by **STEVE BUCHANAN**

Photos:

Cover and pages 31, 45 top, 49, 50, 53, 64, 74, 75, 79, 80 top, 81, 95 by **C. COLSTON BURRELL**

Pages 1, 5, 26, 28, 33, 92 top, 97 bottom, 101 bottom by **JERRY PAVIA**

Pages 6, 9, 19, 23, 37, 39, 76 bottom, 86 bottom, 90 bottom, 92 bottom by **JUDYWHITE**

Pages 15, 29, 35 by **CHRISTINE M. DOUGLAS**

Page 17 by **ALAN L. DETRICK**

Pages 36, 54, 57, 58, 84, 85, 86 top, 87 top, 87 bottom, 90 top, 100 by **SUSAN E. DUMAINE**

Page 43 by **ANDROPOGON ASSOCIATES**

Pages 44 top, 46 top, 80 bottom, 82, 101 top by **ROBERT M. HAYS**

Pages 44 bottom, 45 bottom by **BOB HYLAND**

Page 46 bottom by **FRANK BRAMLEY**

Pages 60, 62 by **ROB PROCTOR**

Pages 67, 96, 97 top by **DANIEL J. HINKLEY**

Pages 69, 71, 72, 99, 102 by **WAYNE WOMACK**

Pages 76 top, 77 by **BRENDA SKARPHOL**

Pages 89, 91 by **ROBERT E. HEAPES**

Page 94 by **JOANNE PAVIA**

INDEX

❦ Gardening Books for the Next Century ❦ from the Brooklyn Botanic Garden

Don't miss any of the gardening books in Brooklyn Botanic Garden's 21st-Century Gardening Series! Published four times a year, these acclaimed books explore the frontiers of ecological gardening—offering practical, step-by-step tips on creating environmentally sensitive and beautiful gardens for the 1990s and the new century. Your subscription to BBG's 21st-Century Gardening Series is free with Brooklyn Botanic Garden membership.

SUBSCRIPTIONS

To become a member, please call (718) 622-4433, ext. 265. Or photocopy this form, complete and return to: Membership Department, Brooklyn Botanic Garden, 1000 Washington Avenue, Brooklyn, NY 11225-1099.

Your name ....

Address ....

City/State/Zip..Phone ....

AMOUNT

☐ Yes, I want to subscribe to the 21st-Century Gardening Series (4 quarterly volumes) by becoming a member of the Brooklyn Botanic Garden:

☐ $35 (Subscriber)   ☐ $125 (Signature Member)

☐ $50 (Partner)   ☐ $300 (Benefactor)   ....

☐ Enclosed is my tax-deductible contribution to the Brooklyn Botanic Garden.   ....

TOTAL   ....

Form of payment: ☐ Check enclosed   ☐ Visa   ☐ Mastercard

Credit card# ....Exp.....................

Signature..

FOR INFORMATION ON ORDERING ANY OF THE FOLLOWING BACK TITLES, PLEASE WRITE THE BROOKLYN BOTANIC GARDEN AT THE ABOVE ADDRESS OR CALL (718) 622-4433, EXT. 274.